God's Lovers

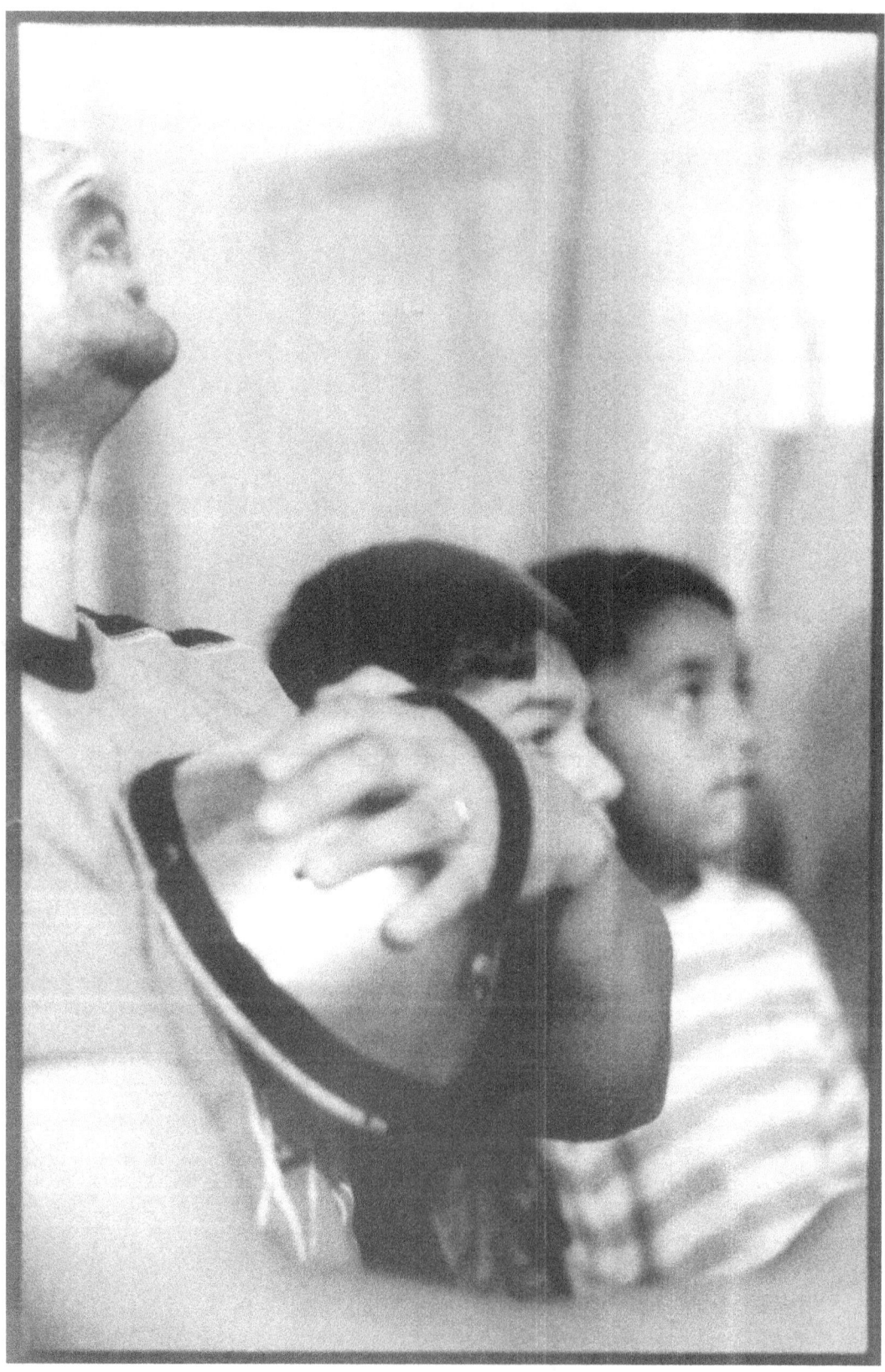

Nicolaas Biegman
Text and Images

God's Lovers

A Sufi Community in Macedonia

Routledge
Taylor & Francis Group
LONDON AND NEW YORK

First published 2007 by
Kegan Paul International

2 Park Square, Milton Park, Abingdon, Oxon OX14 4RN
711 Third Avenue, New York, NY 10017, USA

*Routledge is an imprint of the Taylor & Francis Group,
an informa business*

First issued in paperback 2016

Copyright © 2007 Nicolaas Biegman, text and images

Transferred to Digital Printing 2011

All rights reserved. No part of this book may be reprinted or reproduced or utilised in any form or by any electronic, mechanical, or other means, now known or hereafter invented, including photocopying and recording, or in any information storage or retrieval system, without permission in writing from the publishers.
Notice:
Product or corporate names may be trademarks or registered trademarks, and are used only for identification and explanation without intent to infringe.

British Library Cataloguing in Publication Data
A catalogue record for this book is available from the British Library

ISBN 13: 978-0-7103-1191-7 (hbk)
ISBN 13: 978-1-138-97531-6 (pbk)

Publisher's Note
The publisher has gone to great lengths to ensure the quality of this reprint but points out that some imperfections in the original copies may be apparent. The publisher has made every effort to contact original copyright holders and would welcome correspondence from those they have been unable to trace.

This book is dedicated to the memory of Sheikh Erol, who died on September 16th, 2005.

We, the dervishes, *have accepted the fact that Erol Baba has left us, for now, in this world. From time to time Amdi and I see him in a dream. He says that he is all right and that he is here around us when we work in the* tekke, *that he can see and hear us but that we can't see him. It is strange; if Spielberg heard about this he would at once make a science fiction film about it, but we are actually experiencing it.*

Arben, in an e-mail dated October 14th, 2005

Acknowledgements

I am grateful for the trust and friendship shown me by Erol Baba and his dervishes, who for two years kindly suffered my presence – always with a camera in tow and often extra lighting equipment – at their ceremonies and *muabet*, the friendly conversation that normally follows. The difficult conditions – a small room, lots of motion and emotion and very little light – meant that I often needed supplementary lighting. It was supplied by my close friend and fellow traveler throughout Macedonia, the Macedonian photographer Rumen Kamilov.

Professor Alexandre Popović of CNRS, Paris, generously shared with me his vast knowledge of the Balkan Rifa'is and opened doors to his valuable contacts in the field. I remain indebted to the spirit of Annemarie Schimmel, whose admirable *Mystical Dimensions of Islam* forms the basis for much of the section on Sufism in the Introduction.[1] I also owe a debt of gratitude to the Dutch photographer Bert Nienhuis for teaching me how to use the flash to convey the movement that is so important in Sufi rituals.

Attentive readers may recognize some passages from my previous book on dervishes *Egypt - Moulids, Saints, Sufis* (SDU/Kegan Paul, 1990). The essence of Sufism has not changed over the last fifteen years, so why re-invent the wheel?

A CD with music and *zikr* recorded at the Skopje *tekke* has been released by PAN Records, Leiden, The Netherlands.[2]

Sadly, Baba Erol passed away after I completed the research for this book.

A. Erol Baba standing beside the tomb of Haznadar Baba

Contents

Introduction	1
Photographs	33
List of Names	119
Glossary	121

Photographs A, B and 2-37 were taken between June, 2002 and May, 2004 with a Leica R3 camera.

Photographs 1 and 38-43 were taken in February, 2005 and C and 44-50 on March 22, 2006 with a Nikon D70 digital camera.

Introduction[3]

Within Islam, the Sufis or Dervishes are the gentlest and most tolerant of believers and yet, surprisingly, some adherents thrust iron pins through their cheeks in the course of their devotions. Of course, there is nothing harmful to others in the act of piercing one's own flesh. Besides, it has always been restricted to a small number of Sufi orders and even among these it has become rare. But it is still practiced by the dervishes I knew in Skopje, Macedonia.

At a time when much attention is focused on 'the clash of civilizations' and the violence many perceive to be inherent in Islam, it is helpful to realize that Islam is much more heterogeneous than is often assumed, and that large numbers of Muslims belong to the mystical movement known as Sufism, which is essentially non-political, non-violent and centered on a burning love of God.

If we confine our interest in Islam to the aggressive elements within it – which are undeniably there – we will be unlikely to learn much about the religion *in toto*. The virulent 'Islamists', who use particular interpretations of holy writ to construe their exclusive brand of Islam, are typically noisy and visible, but they are relatively few in number. It is unfortunate that in the West the opinions of this minority are sometimes considered as representative of the spirit of Islam as a whole.

Throughout the Muslim world, from Bosnia to Mozambique and from Senegal to Indonesia, there are thousands of Sufi orders, or *tarikats*. At various times and places, these *tarikats* have played a role in politics, but their theology and approach make them mostly keep to themselves. Their main interest is in God and their relationship with Him, and their cult is built on rituals developed and sustained over many centuries.

God's Lovers is about a marginal group of Roma dervishes with exceptional rituals, living on the fringes of the Islamic world in Macedonia. However, there exist thousands of essentially similar Sufi communities all over the Muslim areas of the globe and there is nothing marginal about them, even though they are often ignored or despised by the elites of their countries. Most are unseen even by orientalists, who have traditionally been trained to study the texts of the literate elites, rather than popular practice. Among Macedonia's Muslims, the Sufis may be few and far between, but in Egypt Sufi orders claim a membership of six million. With the addition of the members of their families, that is a sizeable proportion of the population. In other Muslim countries there is a comparable Sufi presence.

The unassuming mysticism of the Muslim masses has a profound political relevance, as it renders large numbers of believers virtually immune to the recent epidemic of fundamentalism. On the whole, the Sufis don't fight back against the propaganda for a 'pure' faith and the accusations about the supposedly backward and heretical character of their beliefs and practices. They simply close their minds to it. The moderating influence of popular Sufism within the composite and decentralized world of Islam is still far from being fully studied and appreciated.

Sufism demands a life-long commitment. In the words of Yunus Emre[4],

A person who loves God has a heart which never parts from God;
unlike lovers of women, he does not love, then leave.

Usually, though, being a dervish is not a full-time occupation. A *tekke* is not a monastery. As a rule, a dervish has a family and a job (if he can find one), a trade or a profession. Had that not been the case, the Sufi movement would never have attracted so many adherents.

Sufism

The desire to establish an intimate relationship with God is the driving force of the Sufis, the mystics of Islam. Islam does not have a monopoly on mysticism. Love of the Absolute, the great spiritual current which goes through all religions, is a world-wide phenomenon, and the Near East as well as Central Asia had wide experience of both ascetic and Gnostic schools of thought and practice before the advent of Islam.

It can be assumed that the mystical movement in Islam was influenced to some degree by early Christianity and possibly also by Buddhism and Hinduism. Today, though, the prevailing view is that Sufism was essentially an authentic development from within Islam itself, and an important development, as well. At some stage the majority of Muslims may have been affiliated to a Sufi *tarikat*.

Before trying to explain some of the mystical phenomena encountered in Skopje, I would point out that mysticism is action rather than theory, and that no amount of discourse can lead to a mystical experience. As the Persian poet Jami said,

> 'The heir of the Prophet is he who follows the Prophet in his actions, not he who blackens the face of paper.'

In other words, 'Reading about wine does not result in drunkenness.' Moreover, it is no exaggeration to state that Islamic mysticism, especially at the popular level, is a very physical form of spirituality. It follows that one can be a sincere and successful traveller on the mystical Path without being much of an intellectual, let alone exercising one's mind on details of theology. Logically, speaking about the ineffable has its limits. To the Sufi mind, the notion of God and of any relationship a human being may establish with Him can only be intuited, especially through parable, poetry, music and ritual.

This approach differs quite radically from that of the intellectually inclined, orthodox Islamic *'ulama'*, whose views predominate in official modern Islam and whose main occupation is the study of texts and commentaries. This is not to say that a mystic cannot be an Islamic lawyer as well, just as he might combine mysticism with any other profession. Many mystics have had a profound knowledge of the Law, just as many sheikhs of Al-Azhar, up to the nineteenth century, belonged to a Sufi order. But there is an important difference in emphasis between Sufism and Sunni orthodoxy. To the orthodox Muslim, God is first and foremost the Creator, the King and the Judge. The Sufis call Him the Beloved. They are in love with God.

For the mystic, love transcends the Law, and the spirit comes before the letter. Submission *(islam)* to God goes without saying, but love for the Supreme tempers the fear of Him. Fear is only one of the initial 'stations' on the Path, followed in due course by repentance, trust in God, contentment and 'friendship'. This mutual friendship, or love, between God and the individual is by no means easy for the latter to establish, and is ultimately a matter of grace. Sufi songs and poetry refer abundantly to the pain of separation from the Beloved and even to feelings of cruel rejection.

It is held that both the holy texts and religious duties have an outward appearance (*zahir*) and an inner meaning (*batin*). These notions extend to all apparent phenomena, which are believed to be real only up to a point, the real truth (Arabic: *haqiqa*; Turkish: *hakikat*) being with God, the object of direct personal experience or Gnosis (Arabic: *ma'rifa*; Turkish: *marifet*), which can be gained only through specific action, meditation and illumination. Erol Baba, the Sheikh of the Skopje dervishes, said:

> 'The Sunnis[5] occupy themselves with the visible and the tangible (such as daily prayers); the Sufis work on the invisible. That is something one can only feel.'

By the time the first Sufi orders (Arabic: *tariqa*, pl. *turuq*; Turkish: *tarikat*) came into being, Islamic mysticism had been evolving for five hundred years or more. During that time Sufi masters either practised on their own or inspired disciples in groups of varying sizes. The term Sufi derives from the Arabic word *suf*, meaning 'wool', as the mystics were known for the coarse woolen garments they wore. *Darwesh*, which became dervish in Turkish and in English, is the Persian word for 'poor'. The early Sufis usually operated on the margins of society; they were not interested in the world but only in God and, to some degree, in one another. The first appear to have been ascetics, and asceticism remained important in Sufism, if only as a temporary station on the Path. Hasan al-Basri, who died in 728 but is still mentioned in the Skopje rituals, was an example of this kind of mystic. The all-important concept of a pure and disinterested love of God was introduced by Rabi'a al-'Adawiyya (d. 801), a female saint who advocated the love of God for His own sake, not from fear of hell or in hope of paradise. Like all mystics, she aspired to ultimate unity with the Divine.

Dhu-'n-Nun the Egyptian (d. 859) added the notion of *ma'rifa*, Gnosis, an intuitive knowledge of God as distinct from *'ilm*, or discursive learning:

> 'The Gnostics see without knowledge, without sight, without information received and without observation, without description, without veiling and without veil.'

Abu Yazid (Bayezid) Bistami (d. 874) experienced such closeness to God that in a state of rapture he exclaimed, 'Praise be to me!' (*subhani*), much like al-Hallaj (d. 922), who announced, 'I am the Absolute Truth' (*ana' l-haqq*). Hallaj was eventually executed for heresy. At-Tirmidhi (d. early 10th century) contributed the notion of a hierarchy of saints led by the *qutb* or *ghawth*. Later theory added to their number. Junayd of Baghdad (d. 10th century) was a moderate intellectual compared to many Sufis of his time. He is part of most of the initiation chains (*silsilas*) of the present *tarikat*s. Junayd stressed constant purification and mental struggle:

'We did not arrive at Sufism through talk and words, but through hunger and renunciation of the world and of things to which we were accustomed and which we found agreeable.'

He favoured the state of 'sobriety' over the 'intoxication' practised by Bistami and Hallaj. From the year 750, Baghdad was for centuries the center of the Islamic world, so it is not surprising that many of the early Sufi masters lived in Iraq.

'The Greatest Master' (*ash-Shaykh al-Akbar*) Ibn 'Arabi from Murcia (d. Damascus, 1240) codified the teachings of Sufism in large volumes of theoretical prose, and wrote some poetry as well. His main contribution was the notion of the 'one-ness of being (*wahdatu 'l-wujud*)', which essentially means that God is not only everywhere, but also in everything. Ibn 'Arabi visualized the Divine Essence as a vast green ocean from which fleeting forms emerge like waves, only to fall again and disappear in the fathomless depths. Elements of these ideas derived from neo-Platonic speculation. Central to Ibn 'Arabi's system is the veneration of the Prophet Muhammad as the Perfect Man, the medium through whom God is known and manifested.

The almost excessive veneration of the Prophet as the 'friend' or 'beloved', beside God, *par excellence* has remained a characteristic of Sufism. The orthodox Sunnis hold the Prophet in the highest esteem, but rather as God's 'messenger' (*rasulu 'llah*) and the 'seal' of a long line of prophets, even though for them, as well, the imitation of Muhammad is an important objective.

This was the heritage handed down to the *tarikat*s that were established in the twelfth and thirteenth centuries. How this came about is not yet clear. Sufis had tended to congregate in *ribat*s and *khanqah*s, but these were essentially groups of individuals pursuing their own Paths. The *tarikat*s, however, were centered around one individual, a man who initiated followers into his teaching and techniques which were then perpetuated in his name by sheikhs who considered themselves to be his spiritual heirs. Sufi experimentation was confined within the boundaries of each *tarikat*, and it is no wonder that, in this respect, the golden age of Sufism was over. Perhaps it had in any case reached its limits.

The ready recitations of *tarikat* teaching made Sufism, which had hitherto been confined to a select few, accessible to the masses, and whatever was lost in terms of originality was gained in numbers of adherents. The mystical experience was, so to speak, democratized. There had obviously been a widely-felt need for a more intimate and emotional professing of Islam than the orthodox schools could offer. This may have been related to the suppression in Egypt and Iraq of the emotionally expressive Shiite sects. The virtual absence of a central authority in Islam allowed the emergence of parallel institutions of a kind that would never have been tolerated by either the Roman Catholic or the Orthodox churches. Most *tarikats* are Sunni and, as a rule, neither stress the differences between their own and non-Sufi worship nor the differences among themselves.

For the Sufis a highly important means of drawing closer to God is the *zikr*, which is also their most distinctive visible activity. The meaning of the Arabic word *dhikr*, which sounds like *zikr, zikir* or *zikyir* in Turkish and Macedonian, is recollection or remembrance, in this case, the remembrance of God. It is expressed through the recitation of some of the 'most beautiful names' of God, of which there are ninety-nine, and related formulas, typically in a rhythmic chant and often accompanied by corresponding movements of the body. A *zikr* session can begin with a litany called *vird* or *evrad* (Arabic: *wird*, plur. *awrad*), such as the *vird* of Pir Ahmad ar-Rifa'i, which is believed to have special powers. If a senior dervish recites it over a container of water, sipping a little and spitting it back, that water will cure diseases and other ills. In Skopje, this practice has fallen out of favour. Sheikh Erol disapproved of the spitting and instead left bottles of water near the holy tombs to obtain the same result.

Zikr, which takes many forms, is fundamental to Sufi religious practice. According to many Sufis its object is to empty the heart of everything but God. Erol Baba spoke of polishing the heart, enabling the heart and mind to connect with God. He also spoke of concentrating on God, which leads to inspiration. Breath control is a significant element in *zikr*. With the over-simplification one often finds in maxims of this kind, al-Bistami is alleged to have said:

'For Gnostics worship is observance of the breath.'

The repetition of formulaic prayers in the *zikr* is reminiscent of the Jesus Prayer in early Christianity and the *Namu Amida Butsu* in Japanese Buddhism. Contemporary transcendental meditation also resembles it in some respects.

In most *tarikats* the dervishes take part in collective *zikr* sessions at prescribed times which, in some orders, including the Rifa'iyya, are considered superior to individual sessions. They also perform their own *zikr* at home, following a programme ordained by their sheikh. In addition to festive occasions, group *zikrs* are normally held once or twice a week, either at the *tekke* where the founder saint's tomb is located, at a less prestigious *semaana*⁶, or even at someone's home. In Skopje they take place once a week, on Saturday evenings, and last between half an hour and two hours.

Islam has a strong aversion to 'innovation' (*bid'a*), which involves anything that cannot be traced back, at least by analogy, to the Koran or the Prophet's example. It was therefore important to establish precedents for the *zikr* either in the Holy Book or in the collections of traditions or sayings of the Prophet (*hadith*), which were compiled during the first centuries of Islam, particularly because the orthodox have always had reservations about these practices and about Sufism altogether. Fortunately, the Koran is no exception to the rule that in holy books everyone can find what they are looking for, though it is doubtful that the word 'remembrance' (*dhikr*) and the related verb used here were originally applied to what is now called a *zikr*. But apart from that, Sufism developed early enough for a number of the Prophet's sayings on the subject of *zikr* to be included in collections of *hadith* which are considered to be true. A distinct category within the *hadith* embraces the *hadith qudsi*, the sayings that God revealed to the Prophet which were not incorporated in the Koran.

Nine verses of the Koran mention the Remembrance of God, the main injunctions being: 'Remember God with frequent remembrance', 'Remember Me and I shall remember you', and 'After prayers, remember God standing up, seated or (lying) on your side.' The principal text relating to Sufism in *hadith* literature is the *hadith qudsi* commonly called the *hadith an-nawafil*. The Arabic word *nawafil*, the plural of *nafila*, means efforts over and above those prescribed as obligatory such as the five daily prayers. The most important *nafila* is the *zikr*. The text reads:

'My servant draws continually closer to Me by nawafil, until I love him, and when I love him I am the hearing by which he hears, and the sight by which he sees, the hand with which he strikes and the leg on which he walks.'

The *zikr* is additional to the execution of the religious and moral duties incumbent upon all Muslims, whether Sufi or not, such as: 'being just before being generous' and, in the words of an early mystic, 'abstaining from evil before performing pious works', because it is a duty to refrain from all evil whereas no one is obliged to do all good. In short, conventional Islam, including the *'ibadat*, formal duties like the ritual prayers, fasting and pilgrimage, can be seen as a prerequisite for real faith or *iman*, even though 'a mustard seed of love is better than seventy years of worship without love.'

It is also true that prominent masters have advocated a less literal interpretation of the *'ibadat*. Hallaj advised his followers to spend the money they had saved up for the pilgrimage to Mecca on feeding and clothing orphans and making them happy on the day of the Feast. The *Skopski Dervishi* carry out their formal duties in a somewhat selective manner. They strictly observe the Ramadan fast, but the performance of the five daily prayers seems to be a matter for the individual to decide. Some of the dervishes tell me they do the *namaz* according to the *shari'a*, but Erol Baba told me that only the one at dawn was important.

A good dervish is required to cultivate certain qualities and suppress others. As an Egyptian sheikh once told me,

'God loves generosity, especially in the poor, modesty, especially in the rich, and repentance, especially in the young; whereas He abhors stinginess, especially in the rich, arrogance, especially in the poor, and disobedience, especially in the old.'

For the *tarikats* correct behaviour (*edep*; Arabic: *adab*), patience (*sabr*) and hospitality are important values. 'Everything has a servant, and correct behaviour is the servant of religion.' On one of the walls of the *zikr* room in Skopje there is a text in Arabic reading: '*Adab*, oh God' (*adab ya huwa*).

Finally, although Sufis are deeply committed to the precepts of their own *tarikats*, the fact that they are not too much bound by texts and their general approach to the truth have enabled them to accept that many different paths may lead to the Beloved, who resides at the center and belongs to all. This realization has made them tolerant not only of *tarikats* other than their own, but also of other movements within Islam and even other faiths. As Sheikh Osmani put it:

'God is one, but there are faiths by the hundreds.'[7]

No Sufi has ever tried to convert me to his religion.

The Tarikat

A *tarikat* is an 'order' of Sufis who venerate the same founder saint, or *pir*, as the initiator of their 'Path' (the literal meaning of *tariq* or *tariqa* in Arabic), which encompasses their religious beliefs, their rituals and their traditions. Most *tarikats* are named after their founder: the Qadiriyya after Abdul Qadir al-Jilani, the Naqshbandiyya after Baha' ad-Din Naqshband, the Mevleviya, or Mawlawiyya after Mevlana Jelal ed-Din Rumi, the Bektashiyya after Haji Bektash Veli, and the Rifa'iyya, the *tarikat* of the dervishes of Skopje, after Pir, or Sheikh, Ahmad ar-Rifa'i. One exception is the Halveti order, or Khalwatis, who take their name from the *halvet* (Arabic: *khalwa*), the place for solitary worship, which plays an important role on their Path. The orders can be roughly divided into two categories: the 'urban' category who have a more refined ritual, and the 'rustic' orders who have rather exuberant practices which sometimes include the piercing of certain parts of the body. The Mevlevis, who are well known in the West for the exquisite music and elegant whirling displayed most notably at Konya in Turkey, are an urban order *par excellence*. The Rifai's and the Sa'dis are examples of rustic *tarikats*. Some *tarikats* identify themselves by means of a distinctive colour. For the Rifa'iyya that colour is black, though white is used as well.

A *tarikat* comprises many highly independent groups, each headed by a sheikh or *baba* who, spiritually at least, wields absolute power over his followers. To the best of my knowledge, and certainly in the case of the Rifa'is, the various groups and branches of a *tarikat* are not linked by a central authority beyond the borders of the state in which they live, and even within those borders the sheikhs are fiercely independent. Sheikhs in the same region, say, in Macedonia and Kosovo, maintain ties with one another, but have so little contact with their counterparts in the Arab world that with time significant differences can and, indeed, do occur. As a result, different *tarikats* in the same region may have more in common with one another in terms of ritual and doctrine than with members of their own *tarikat* in other parts of the Muslim world. One example is the singing of hymns or *ilahis*, which is unknown among the Egyptian Sufis I know, but is common among the Turks and is also nowadays practiced in Macedonia both by the Rifa'is and the Halvetis. This element of the ritual appears to have been borrowed from Christian sects in Anatolia when their members converted to Islam[8], and seems to occur only in Turkey and the Balkans.

The Rifa'iyya, or Rufa'iyya as they call themselves in Macedonia, are one of the largest and most active *tarikats* in the world, especially at the popular level. Up to the sixteenth century they were the most geographically dispersed of the Sufi orders. Though overtaken in that respect by the Qadiriyya, they are still active in Egypt, Iraq, Syria, Turkey, around the Indian Ocean and in the Balkans, where their centers are in Kosovo and Macedonia.

The order was established by one of the earliest *tarikat* founders, Sidi Ahmad ar-Rifa'i. In Skopje the dervishes call him called *Hazreti Pir* (His Eminence the Sheikh).

Rifa'i (1106-1182) lived in the marshlands of southern Iraq, which he left only once in order to go on pilgrimage to Mecca and Medina, but still attracted many Sufis to his retreat in the village of Umm 'Abida, or Umm 'Ubayda. Sidi Ahmad was a descendant of the Prophet through both his parents, whose family trees could be traced back to Muhammad's grandsons Husayn and Hasan, respectively, hence his name, *Abu 'l-'Alamayn*, the Man with the Two Flags. He was neither a writer - although the *tarikat*'s special litany is attributed to him - nor an original thinker. His fame may be attributed to his extraordinary personality. Right from the start, and probably taking an example from the founder himself, his *tarikat* was known for its passion and flamboyance. Its members performed feats like riding lions, walking on burning coals, and piercing their bodies with iron. In Egypt and some other countries, although not in Macedonia, the Rifa'i dervishes are credited with power over scorpions and snakes.

In Rifa'i's time, Islam along with Christianity, Manichaeism and vestiges of many older creeds, coexisted in the marshlands. Their proximity to one another may have endowed Rifa'i's followers with a measure of doctrinal flexibility which enabled them to assimilate concepts that can be regarded as somewhat heterodox.

Although the Rifa'iyya were present in Turkey quite early on, and the travel writer Evliya Çelebi mentions Rifa'is in Macedonia in the mid-seventeenth century, there is little evidence of their presence in the Balkans before the nineteenth century. The *tarikat* was introduced, or re-introduced, into Macedonia in 1818, when the founder of the Skopje branch, Mehmed Baba Haznadar, who had been initiated by a visiting sheikh from an Arab country, possibly Egypt, founded the present *tekke*. Until recently, this group was dominated by ethnic Turks.

The predominantly Albanian branch was founded in 1860 by Sheikh Musa, who had been initiated in Istanbul. He established the *tekke* in Gjakova/Djakovica in Kosovo, from whence the *tarikat* spread to Prizren, Rahovec/Orahovac and other Kosovan towns, then to various parts of Albania, and eventually to Bosnia.

The Macedonian and Kosovan Rifa'is are in close contact. Erol Baba 'took the hand' from Sheikh Baki, meaning he was made a sheikh by him at Orahovac, and remained attached to him up to the time of Baki's death. Likewise, Erol Baba's son and successor, Murtezan, 'took the hand' from Sheikh Mehdi, the son of Sheikh Baki. Brethren from Orahovac regularly attend *zikr* sessions at the Skopje *tekke*. The *lingua franca* between the two groups is Serbian, or Bosnian as they prefer to call it.

The Rifa'i *tarikat* in Macedonia has certainly seen better days. A predominantly Turkish organization, its numbers declined substantially during the Turkish emigration that started in 1912 and peaked in the 1950s. Had it not been for the Romas' sudden, massive interest in the *tarikat*, the Macedonian Rufa'iyya might have disappeared altogether. I am not certain why or exactly when the Macedonian Romas became involved in the *tarikat*. I have heard that Sheikh Xhemali of the Rifa'i *tekke* in Prizren, Kosovo, who died in 2003 or 2004, was engaged in some proselytizing among them. In any case, it seems that the emotional and rather informal style of Sufi worship is attractive to many Romas. Their low status as an ethnicity may have prevented them from joining earlier, when the *tekke* in Skopje was still a solidly Turkish institution. As it is, with the new Roma members, numbers are increasing steadily. There are now thirteen or fourteen *semaanas* in the Skopje region, notably in the Roma township of Shutka, and ten in other parts of the country. Erol Baba authorized their establishment and remained their sheikh but, for the rest, let them be. According to his estimate, each *semaana* could count up to fifty dervishes. This means there might now be over a thousand Rifa'is in Macedonia, possibly as many as there ever were.

In the Balkans and Egypt, and no doubt elsewhere, the followers of the Rifa'iyya have always been drawn from the lower and lower middle classes. The *tarikat*'s unbridled practices hold little appeal for the Muslim bourgeoisie. Even so, the Rifa'is are respected by the other *tarikats*, including the very disciplined Halvetis of Struga, who follow Sunni doctrine but pursue the same objective as diligently as the Rifa'is, albeit in their own fashion. Each *tarikat* has its own way in which its adherents move from the Law (*sheriat*) through the Order (*tarikat*) to Gnosis (*marifet*) and, ultimately, to God's Truth (*hakikat*).

Apart from certain doctrinal aspects, the main characteristic of the Macedonian Rifa'is is the intense passion expressed during the *zikr*, which involves the piercing of cheeks, throat and other parts of the body without any blood flowing. According to Erol Baba, the practice of piercing is neither a goal in itself nor a means of achieving a goal; it is an expression of the spiritual state the dervishes reach during the ritual. He said,

'We pierce ourselves when love takes hold of us (kad nas hvata ljubav),'

It shows the dervishes and any doubters what God's love and power can achieve. This may be one reason why there is nothing secret about the piercing or about the *zikr* as a whole, even though the sheikh has to give permission for visitors, whether male or female, to attend.

At one stage I noticed that the piercing had not been practised for some time, and I asked Erol Baba the reason. 'You may remember,' he replied, 'that three weeks ago some bleeding occurred. I think it was because some women had come in and watched the *zikr* without asking. Haznadar Baba, the saint who is buried in the *tekke*, does not like that. So I decided to suspend the piercing for a month or so.' It was resumed soon afterwards.

Baba Erol was proud of this custom, though he no longer applied the *zarp* to himself. He enjoyed showing a video in which a Kurdish dervish performing a *zikr* had a knife hammered into his skull by his sheikh, and he was sad to learn that the *darb as-silah* had become very rare in Egypt. Piercing is done either with a *t'g*, a thin metal pin inserted by the sheikh, or a *zarp*, a thicker, sharp iron implement which has a wooden ball on one side to which small iron chains are attached. In most cases, the dervish receives the *zarp* from the sheikh and inserts it himself.

In terms of doctrine, the Rifa'is of Skopje occupy a position somewhere between their orthodox Sunni brethren in Egypt and the Bektashis and Alevis of the Balkans, who are Shiites, though not of the kind prevalent in Iran. This is consistent with the view, expressed in 1934 by Sheikh Qazim Peja in Shkodra, that the Rifa'iyya is midway between Sunnism and Bektashism.[9] According to Erol Baba, Ali's heirs are the Shia, the Alevis and the dervishes and their *tarikats*.[10] He also believed that Ali and Muhammad are one. This is clearly expressed in the following lines from one of the group's *ilahi* songs:

> 'Muhammad is Ali, Ali-Muhammad,
> Ali is Muhammad, Ali-Muhammad, Allah!
> Ali is Muhammad, Ali-Muhammad.'[11]

Baba Erol used to quote a *hadith* in which, according to his interpretation, the Prophet says about Ali:

'His word is my word, his body is my body, his blood is my blood, his spirit is my spirit.'

Repeated in the *zikr* a number of times is the phrase: 'God! Bless our Lord Muhammad and Ali-Muhammad!'[12]

The Bektashis postulate a continuum between Muhammad and Ali, and believe in a trinity consisting of God, Ali and Muhammad. The Skopje *tekke* contains numerous images of Ali and a decorative inscription of the names of the Bektashi trinity. There is an image of the twelve Imams seated in a row, which I also saw at Orahovac and in the

Bektashi *tekke* in Tetovo. The Rifa'is of Orahovac have a long *ilahi* song in Albanian about each of the twelve Shiite Imams. The number twelve recurs in a prayer in the *zikr* for the souls of 'the twelve Imams and the twelve Pirs.'[13] And the *taj* (cap) worn by the Skopje sheikhs has twelve furrows like that of the Bektashi babas. As the well-known Rifa'i Sheikh Xhemali from Prizren put it in an interview, 'We belong to the Sunni school of Islam, but we believe in the same things as the Shiites.'[14]

The main feasts in Skopje are Shiite, as well. These include Ashura on the tenth of the Islamic month of Muharram, preceded by a twelve-day fast (*matem*), which commemorates the death of Ali's son Husayn at Kerbela, and Sultan Nevruz, the Persian New Year, which is believed to be the birthday of *Hazret-i Ali*, on 21 March and following days. The *matem* is a period of mourning throughout which no festivity, music or sexual intercourse is allowed.

The performance of prayers before dawn, in Sheikh Erol's words 'the hour when all doors open,' also recalls the Bektashis who perform prayers at dawn and sunset only. However, pre-dawn prayers are also common in some of the more orthodox orders such as the Khalwatiyya. Erol Baba referred to Iraq as a cursed place, because that is where they killed al-Husayn.

The syncretization of Sunni and Shiite beliefs in this part of the Balkans does not come as a surprise since, until recently and especially at the popular level, syncretization extended even to Christianity. As the saying went, 'Ali until midday, Elijah after midday' (*do podne Alija, popodne Ilija*.) In fact, various ethnic groups were largely indifferent to religious doctrine. Indeed, the Albanians have always been known for this. People would proclaim themselves either Christian or Muslim depending on the circumstances and on the person they were speaking to, and they still visit each other's saints depending on the saint's particular powers.

Compared to what it might have been, the heterodoxy of the Macedonian Rifa'is is relatively mild. It certainly does not prevent the sheikh from maintaining official relations with the very 'Sunni' leadership of the Islamic Community of Macedonia headed by the Reis ul-Ulema, who respects his autonomy. Within the Islamic Community, Sheikh Erol was the nominal head of the *tarikat*s in Macedonia.

The Sheikh

The sheikh (Persian: *pir*; Turkish: *baba*; Macedonian: *sheh*) is the defining personality in the *tarikat*. As the head of a group of Sufis, the sheikh is responsible for the transmission of the order's wisdom to the next generation of dervishes. Through the *silsila*, the chain that connects him to all his predecessors and ultimately to Ali and the Prophet, he carries the light that illuminates his followers' Path. He has absolute authority over his disciples both before and after their initiation. In relation to his sheikh, a dervish is 'like a corpse in the hands of the washer of the dead.' Just as the sheikh looks after all the spiritual and often other needs of the dervish, the dervish owes absolute loyalty and respect to his sheikh. He presses his forehead to the palm of the sheikh's hand and kisses it and occasionally bows at his feet with his forehead touching the ground. In addition to the 'horizontal solidarity' among the brethren, this vertical solidarity between the sheikh and each one of them is essential for the cohesion of the group.

The sheikh's *taj*, or 'crown', is a white twelve-furrowed felt cap with a black turban wound around it. When at work in the *tekke*, the sheikh wears a long black robe (*jubbe*) over his clothes. He also has a green *jubbe* for special occasions, but I never saw him wear it. The sheikh's 'throne' is a sheepskin (*post*, a Persian word) which lies on the ground in a corner of the room where the *zikr* is held.

The position of sheikh normally passes to a son, the *shehzade*, or another member of the family. If this is not possible, a successor is chosen on the basis of merit. The death of a sheikh is often followed by a bitter dispute over succession among his sons or other relatives. The Rifa'i *tekke* at Orahovac was embroiled in an altercation of this kind for some time after the death of Sheikh Baki, and a similar conflict at the Bektashi *tekke* in Kanatlarci has split the community in two.

Until recently the sheikh of the Rifa'i *tekke* in Skopje was Erol, known, for reasons of language and preference, as Sheikh Erol, Baba Erol or, in line with Turkish usage, Erol Baba. He was born as Ibrahim Murteza. In 1988 he succeeded his father Haydar Baba who was the son of the first sheikh from the Murteza family to take over as the *tekke*'s baba after the death in 1936 of the last descendant of Haznadar Baba, the original founder of the *tekke*. On his father's death, Ibrahim was made a sheikh by Sheikh Baki in Orahovac. He changed his name to Erol, and became the head of the *tekke*.

Erol Baba, who was married with two sons and a daughter and lived next door to the *tekke*, was deeply aware of his status as one of the few prominent ethnic Turks left in the capital. He too had considered leaving for Turkey, but had decided not to give in. He appeared not to mind that the vast majority of his dervishes were Roma now. Ethnicity is not an issue in the *tarikat*, he used to say.

After suffering a mild stroke, Sheikh Erol fell seriously ill in September 2003 and underwent a triple bypass operation. The surgeon advised him not to take part in the ceremonies for a while. As a result, attendance at the *zikr*, which was conducted by two alternating *vekils* in his absence, fell off to some extent, but there was no imminent threat to the group's survival. Erol Baba resumed his duties at the building containing the holy tombs, the *turbe,* assisting supplicants visiting the *kubur* of Haznadar Baba, and as of June, 2005 again attended parts of the *zikr*. In the beginning of September of that year he suffered a massive stroke, and he died on the sixteenth of the same month, still in his fifties. The next day he was buried in the *turbe*. His son Murtezan took over as head of the *tekke* some six months later.

Like many Sufi sheikhs I have met, Erol Baba combined absolute seriousness in his spiritual work with a healthy sense of humour and a complete lack of pomposity in his daily life. When at home he behaved in an utterly unassuming manner, and he showed his visitors the cordial and uncomplicated hospitality which is still the rule in this region of the Balkans. He enjoyed showing up in his 'uniform,' as he called it, at diplomatic receptions, thus causing mild surprise among the guests.

As we became better acquainted, he was willing to speak in more depth about the *tarikat* and to explain the meaning of the rituals and the goings-on around the holy tombs. Half in jest he compared me with Rumi and himself with Shams Tabrizi, Rumi's initiator and source of inspiration.

He didn't hide his wife Naime or his daughter Sema, and was critical of Sheikh Baki of Orahovac, whom he otherwise greatly respected, for hiding his womenfolk. That was the Albanian way, he used to say. The Turks were more liberal.

The Dervishes

Like people everywhere, Sufis tend to acquire their religion from their parents. Fathers bring their sons to the *zikr* as soon as they can walk. Boys of eight or ten take part in the ceremony and, when the sheikh feels they are ready, he pierces their cheeks with a *t'g*. As Arben, one of the dervishes, explained, 'children participate in the *zikr* because before

B. Children start participating in the *zikr* at an early age

God they are the same as us adults.' The condition is that whoever takes part in the *zikr* has a strong desire, or *ashk* (Ar.: *'ashq*, a deep longing, or love), to do so, and is not moved by any other reason. It has to be voluntary and with the consent of the parents. There is no exact minimum age to become an *ashik* (Ar.: *'ashiq*, 'a lover;' meaning someone who is preparing to become a dervish) or a dervish. Some try all their lives without success, and for some it is easy. It all depends on their *ashk* and love for the *tarikat* and, of course, for God. One cannot become a dervish overnight, for there is a period of uncertain duration during which the candidate must go through certain trials to prove his real character. The sheik follows and knows all about the initiate's progress. There are cases in which someone comes on his own account and asks the sheikh to make him a dervish. This man too must go through certain trials. If and when he is successful he 'obtains the hand' from the sheikh, that is to say, he becomes a dervish. Sometimes, as happened during my stay in Skopje, a devotee has a dream telling him to join the *tarikat*, and he goes through the same procedure.

Erol Baba told me that an *ashik* performs manual labor in the *tekke* and the garden for a year or so ('the more he works, the better') supervised by a senior dervish who acts as his guide, or *rehber*. He then spends a few months studying the prayers, litanies and *ilahi*s, after which he is inaugurated as a *muhib* (Arabic: *muhibb*, also meaning 'lover').

Initiations take place in the *zikr oda*. Twelve candles are lit on the floor. The dervishes are seated in a circle, with the sheikh on his *post*, when the new dervish is admitted and introduced by two of the brethren. On entering, the postulant says, 'Greetings, people of the Law'. The group responds with the words: 'Greetings to you, as well.' The postulant says, 'Greetings, people of the *Tarikat*,' to which the group replies in the same manner. The newcomer subsequently addresses the group as 'people of Gnosis' and 'people of the Truth'.[15] He then sits before the sheikh, who prays with him, girds him with the belt (*kemer*), places a *kule* on his head, and whispers the 'secret' (*sirr*) in his ear. The *sirr*, Erol Baba explained, consists mainly of ethical advice:

'Watch your hands, your loins and your tongue (eline, beline, diline)'.

These are the organs with which people can inflict harm on themselves and others. The sheikh also tells him that obeying the rules of the *tarikat* is beneficial, but warns that disobedience is punished by God.

A few years later the *muhib* achieves the status of a fully-fledged dervish, or *dede*. The difference between a *muhib* and a *dede* is reflected in the 'homework' or individual *zikr* prescribed by the sheikh. This *zikr,* which is sometimes called the *tespih* prayer (*tespih namaz*), must be performed at home once every twenty-four hours, using a rosary made of one hundred beads (*tesbih* or *tespih;* Arabic: *tasbih*). The best time is at the end of the night before the call to attend the dawn prayer. One *ilahi* written in Turkish by Haydar Baba and still sung today has the refrain, 'Arise for the *tespih namaz* (*kalk tespih namazina*).' *Muhib*s and *dede*s recite their formulas between fifty and a hundred times, but the *muhib* has only three formulas to recite, whereas the *dede* has five and the sheikh adds one longer formula, which counts for another two.[16]

The sheikh assigns clearly defined responsibilities and tasks to his dervishes. In Skopje, Yashar and Albert take turns in assuming the role of *vekil* and leading the *zikr* in the sheikh's absence. Two *turbedars*, Arben and Amdi, look after the holy tombs. One dervish, with the help of an assistant, is in charge of the *kafe odžak* (making tea or coffee and serving the guests); one acts as doorkeeper; one cleans and polishes the *zarps* and *t'gs* used for piercing; one takes care of the musical instruments; one looks after the garden, and one arranges the shoes that worshippers leave at the entrance.

At the *tekke* at Orahovac in Kosovo, the congregation is much larger than in Skopje. Besides the *rehber,* there are two older dervishes with special functions connected with initiation ceremonies called *bayraktars*, or standard bearers.

The Tekke

A *tekke* (Arabic: *takiyya*) is the center in which a Sufi community and their sheikh congregate to perform their rituals. It often contains the tomb of its founder, who is venerated as a saint. The Rifa'i *tekke* in Skopje is situated in the old Turkish quarter of Gazi Baba, not far from the mosque of Ya(h)ya Pasha. It consists of two low, whitewashed buildings arranged in an L-shape, facing a yard in which there are ancient graves and a well. The main building houses the ceremonial *semaana,* a beautiful domed hall built of wood, where the *zikr* is held on feast days when a relatively large number of people attend. It also contains the guest room or *misafir oda*, where the books and manuscripts are kept, a small *kafe odžak,* where coffee and tea are made, and the *zikr* room, the *zikr oda,* where the regular *zikrs* take place. The *zikr oda* is also called the *post oda,* after the sheikh's sheepskin.

The second building, the *turbe,* is an elongated structure adjacent to the main building. It houses the tomb of the founder saint and those of a further ten sheikhs, along with four of their sisters or wives and one dervish whose name was Abdal. There are sixteen tombs in all, neatly arranged in three rows. Each *kubur* is covered with a green cloth. Outside in the yard are the graves of another ten sheikhs and dervishes and some of their wives or female relatives.

The complex dates from the first half of the nineteenth century, but has undergone various alterations and repairs. It is recognized as a cultural monument by the Macedonian government. The sheikh's living quarters are next door to the *lekke*, behind a garden with a gate leading on to the *tekke* grounds.

The Saint

The tomb of the *tekke*'s founder saint, Mehmed Baba Haznadar, usually called Haznadar Baba, is located in the *turbe*. It is situated at the head of the middle row of tombs, to the right of the entrance.

Besides the numerous objects left by visitors, there are four thousand-bead rosaries in the *turbe*. Three hang from wooden posts near Haznadar's tomb and one lies on the tomb itself. The rosaries are passed over the heads or bodies of those seeking assistance from the saint. There is also a Koran and, behind the tomb, the antlers of a deer that is said to have offered itself as a sacrificial animal by entering the *tekke* grounds about one hundred and fifty years ago. On the walls are portraits of Ali and a picture of him on horseback, brandishing his two-pronged sword *Dhu 'l-Fiqar*.

In theory, a Sufi might be able to find his Path by relying on his master alone, without the help of saints. But in popular contemporary Sufism it is impossible to dissociate this endeavor from the cult of the 'Friends of God.' Someone who joins a *tarikat* becomes part of a spiritual network which extends from his sheikh to the group's founder saint and embraces numerous other saints, including the founders of the *tarikats*, the members of the Prophet's immediate family and descendants (*ehl-i beyt*, Arabic: *ahl al-bayt*, meaning 'the people of (his) house'), and ultimately the Prophet himself. The dervish names them in his prayers during the *zikr* and asks for their support, *meded* (Arabic: *madad*).

The phenomenon of the 'holy man', one who has intimate knowledge of God and who can act, especially after his death, as an intermediary between man and God, is common to a number of religions. In Christianity, the hierarchies of the Roman Catholic and Orthodox churches recognize a multitude of saints on the basis of elaborate rules. Only Protestantism repudiates the concept of saints, stressing instead the direct relationship between man and God without the intervention of anyone or anything. In this respect, orthodox Sunni Islam resembles Protestantism. According to Sunni doctrine, God's message delivered through the Prophet and the Prophet's example evident from his 'customs' (*sunna*), duly interpreted by the '*ulama*', provide Muslims with a complete set of rules to study and observe. Further intercession between man and God is neither necessary nor possible. All that the believer has to do is to obey the Divine Law. Prayers are said, but no personal response can be expected. Nor is there any special enlightenment to be found in this world. One studies the rules, applies them faithfully, and counts on a reward in the hereafter.

Mass Sufism originated from the feeling that in the approach championed by the '*ulama*', the distance between humble mortals and transcendent God was too great, and that a certain degree of intimacy, both with God and with the spirit of the Prophet, should be possible. Particularly at the popular level, there was and still is a perceived need for an intermediary between man and God, just as an ordinary citizen does not expect to have access to a Head of State, but consults an official or a lawyer. This is how the cult of the saints came about in Islam, as in other religions. It also happened that converts to Islam perpetuated this custom, substituting Muslim saints for Christian ones or for Hindu gods. In the *Verse of the Throne* (Sura II, 255) the Koran hints at the possibility of intercession, 'Who will intercede in His (i.e., God's) presence except as He permitteth?' Accordingly, the saints are those who are allowed by God to intercede, along with the Prophet and his family.

There is no hierarchy of priests in Sunni Islam. Any righteous Muslim with some knowledge of the Koran and the ritual can be a *hodža* or *imam* and lead the prayers or deliver a Friday sermon. The Islamic communities are organized on a nationwide rather than international basis, and the authority of the national *ra'is ul-'ulama*'s is more often than not of a predominantly administrative nature. Hence there is no effective authority either to canonize or deconsecrate saints. Apart from that, the orthodox Sunni leaders are not much interested in saints as such. Accordingly, the recognition of saints is largely a local matter.

Apart from Saudi Arabia, whose puritanical regime has systematically destroyed all holy tombs other than that of the Prophet, the Muslim countries are dotted with the domes of *turbe*s, *mazar*s and *maqam*s. These shrines which may, but need not, contain a saint's mortal remains, are sites to which people go in search of healing, blessing and succor. The saint is held to maintain a non-corporeal presence within the tomb. Sheikh

Erol told me that the authorities once ordered a saint's tomb to be destroyed in order to make room for another building. His father, Haydar Baba, claimed and was allowed to take personal care of the demolition together with his son to make sure that the saint's remains would be handled with due respect. When they opened the tomb, Erol felt the saint's spirit, the *ruh*, touching his cheek. A saint is revered and his tomb is visited as long as he or she is perceived to perform the intercession (*shefaat*; Arabic: *shafa'a*) and the miracles (*keramet*; Arabic: *karama*, pl. *karamat*) that are expected from him. Once this perception stops, the cult withers away.

Several passages of the Koran refer to 'friends' (Arabic: *wali*, pl. *awliya'*; Turkish: *veli* or *evliya*, both used in the singular) of God, but they are not entrusted with special responsibilities. According to the Koran, neither the past nor the future bothers them; the *awliya' Allah* know neither fear nor grief. The term *wali* subsequently came to mean 'saint', so that these passages from the Koran, supplemented by traditions (*hadith*) surrounding the Prophet and his contemporaries, provided a legal basis for the cult of saints in Islam.

One such *veli* is Haznadar Baba who, according to local tradition, while serving as treasurer (*haznadar* or *hazinedar*) of Skopje, was initiated into the Rifa'i *tarikat* in 1816. He founded the *tekke* in 1818. The cult of Haznadar Baba is very important in the life of the dervishes of Skopje. They remember Haznadar Baba at various stages of the *zikr*, they end the *zikr* with a special prayer directed towards his tomb, and they regularly visit the *turbe* to pray at his *kubur*. Ahead of a visit, or *ziyaret*, they perform their ablutions as they would for the daily prayers. Two *turbedars* clean the *turbe* thoroughly once a week, before the Saturday *zikr*. 'Haznadar Baba,' the *turbedar* Amdi says, 'gives you everything you ask for – health, a job, brains (*fikir*), peace in the family – as long as you have love in your heart.'

Besides being a holy place for the dervishes, Haznadar's tomb attracts a steady stream of supplicants of all faiths. They are admitted to the tomb by the sheikh, who keeps the *turbe* under lock and key. He helps them approach the saint with their problems, which may be of any kind: health, love and potency, unemployment, the loss of an object, or envy (*hased*; Arabic: *hasad*). Baba Erol used to say,

'Envy does lots of damage, and it is better to be pitied than envied. Envy is merciless.'

Baba Erol could identify the source of the envy afflicting a visitor. He wrote amulets (*amayliya*) to protect the person against it or against other types of ill. If something valuable had been stolen, he sometimes gave the visitor some dust (*dževher*) from the tomb, to be left at the place where the stolen object was last seen. The thief would feel compelled to return it.[17]

Whenever he has a serious problem, the visitor may offer the saint a *kurban*, a sacrificial lamb that is killed in his honour and whose meat is then distributed among the poor.

There are also vows and pledges. Haznadar Baba is loved, but he is feared as well. 'There is no joking with Haznadar Baba' (*so Haznadar Baba nema šhala*), Erol Baba used to say in his mixture of Serbian and Macedonian. Even after completing the virtuous act of cleaning the *turbe* each week, the *turbedars* pray fervently for forgiveness for any mistake they may unwittingly have made in the course of their duties. The saint punishes those who make empty promises, whether by failing to make a pledged sacrifice or to keep a vow made at the tomb, for instance to stop smoking or drinking. A vow taken in the *turbe* therefore strengthens a person's resolve, and people are willing to pay for that.

The sheikh's services at the tomb are not free of charge, nor could they be, since there is hardly any other source of income for the *tekke* or for himself and his family. On the whole the dervishes have very little to spend. After the *zikr* the sheikh often pays for their transport back to their homes in the outlying areas.

Baba Erol had full confidence in Haznadar Baba, who had never abandoned him in times of need. The saint appeared to him in a vision shortly before his operation and told him not to worry. After the operation Baba Erol remained in a coma for two weeks, but finally regained consciousness, much to the surprise of his doctors and nurses. Whenever he was short of money, he told me, 'some gypsy would turn up to make a vow and leave a few hundred marks.'

Haznadar Baba's tomb is the most potent of those in the *turbe*, but other *kuburs* have some *kudret* as well. Bottles of water are placed on the ridge of the tomb of Erol Baba's father, Haydar Baba, and left there for two or three days in order to obtain blessing (*bereket*; Arabic: *baraka*). However, Haznadar's tomb attracts more visitors than any other. It is covered with the garments and towels of supplicants who will return to retrieve them and use them for healing or other purposes once they have absorbed the saint's *bereket*. The tomb is surrounded by plastic bags containing various objects which are left there for a few days for the same purpose.

Among the Rifa'is of Macedonia and Kosovo there does not appear to exist a custom of holding festive annual celebrations *('mawalid')* in the honour of saints, well known in Egypt and other Muslim countries.

The Ritual

The *zikr* room measures roughly four by five meters. Apart from the rugs that cover the floor there is no furniture. The focal point is the corner with the Sheikh's *post*, the sheepskin on which only he is allowed to sit. The *post* is not used by anyone else in his absence and whoever leads the *zikr* as *vekil* or *zakirbashi* sits beside it. The *zarps* and *t'gs* used for piercing are kept in the corner behind the *post*, where the sheikh can reach them when they are needed.

To start a *zikr* the dervishes sit in a circle, or *halka* (Arabic: *halqa*), which includes the sheikh on his *post*. As in the other *zikr*s I have seen, whether conducted in a circle or, as in Egypt, in long rows with the participants facing one another, the ceremony is not oriented in any particular direction as is the case in regular Muslim prayers, which are directed towards the Ka'ba in Mecca. At the end of a session, a prayer is said facing the tomb of Haznadar Baba, but by then the *zikr* as such is already over.

The session can last between thirty minutes and two hours. It comprises a fixed sequence of procedures, many of which were described by Liliana Mašulović-Marsol in 1981.[18] Within that scheme the leader has a certain measure of latitude. I have attended dozens of *zikr*s, and no two were exactly the same. What they all had in common was the degree of passion with which the dervishes performed their ritual. Their communal recitation of the Koran and the 'ejaculatory litanies'[19] and hymns (*ilahis*) are visibly and audibly charged with emotion. Watching a *zikr* can be an impressive experience. Most of the *zikr* is recited or sung at full voice, with the participants sometimes accompanying themselves on *def*s (tambourines) or *kudum*s (metal bowls covered with a skin and beaten with a piece of leather).[20] The leader may use a *zil* (cymbals) to mark the rhythm and indicate the transition to the following section.

A session typically starts with the singing of rhythmic *ilahi*s as a means of warming up. The Skopje dervishes have a repertoire of hymns in Arabic, the liturgical language of Islam; in Turkish, until recently the dominant language within the group, in Serbian or Bosnian, the regional *lingua franca*, and in Romany, which is the mother tongue of most of the dervishes today. Naturally, hardly any one of them, not even the lead singer, Amdi, knows all four languages. It follows that from time to time they sing songs with a text of which they have only a vague understanding, but this doesn't seem to bother them. [21]

The first Romany songs were introduced, with the sheikh's permission, around 1995. Since most of the dervishes are now Roma, the number of Romany songs is likely to increase. For similar reasons, the dervishes in Orahovac use Albanian in most of their *ilahi*s. The use of the vernacular is consistent with the linguistic flexibility that has always been a Sufi characteristic. At times when Arabic and Persian were the official languages in Anatolia, Central Asia and the Indian subcontinent, Sufi preachers and poets such as Yunus Emre expressed themselves in local languages which helped to foster both the development of those languages and the spread of Islam. In present-day Egypt, Sufi singers often use the country's various dialects. Some groups in Europe and North America use English.

After the *ilahis* a candle is lit in the center of the *halka*. The dervishes prostrate themselves, saying '*hu-hu-hu*' (Arabic: *huwa*, meaning He, i.e. God), and silently recite the *niyet* (Arabic: *niyya*, 'intention'), the expression of sincerity which, Erol Baba explains, unites them with Hazreti Pir, the founder of the *tarikat*. They then resume a sitting position. The leader asks God's forgiveness[22] and pronounces the profession of faith: 'There is no god but God, Muhammad is the messenger of God.'[23] All recite together the last three chapters of the *Koran* and the first, the *Fatiha*. The rhythmic part of the *zikr* then begins and the dervishes sway to the left and right beating their *def*s and *kudum*s and repeating various formulas which they call *esma*s (Arabic: *asma'*, i.e., 'names'), all in Arabic, each lasting for a few minutes at the sheikh's discretion. The first is always, as in Egypt, *la ilaha illa 'llah*, ('There is no god but God'). At a sign of the sheikh, the dervishes may articulate the *esma*s like four short barks. Hence the epithet the Rifa'is acquired in the nineteenth century, when they were known in European circles as 'the howling dervishes'. After this they intone *esma*s like *Allah, ya Allah* (God, oh God); *hayy- hayy- hayy* (living) *Allah*; *hu-hu-hu-hu; ya hayy; hayy-hayy-hayy-hayy; da'im haqq Allah hay*[24] and 'You are the Guide, You are the Truth, no one is the Guide but He.'

If time is limited, the entire *zikr* can be performed seated. Normally, however, the dervishes rise at a signal from the leader, remove the candle and put on the light. In this standing or '*kiyami*' phase, the movements are more free, though conditioned by the forceful rhythm, which stays the same throughout the ceremony. The participants mostly remain in the same spot, but occasionally some start moving slowly counter-clockwise while forming an inner circle. Two or four of them may join hands and do a much quicker counter-clockwise *devran* (Arabic: *dawaran*, 'a going round') in the center. *Ilahis* are sung, usually by Amdi or Yashar, while the group continues to beat their instruments and to chant the *esma*s, especially *la ilaha illa 'llah*.

Piercing is usually done during the chanting of *hayy-hayy-hayy-hayy* or *hayy-hayy-hayy Allah*. Anyone who feels the urge approaches the sheikh with his arms crossed over his chest. The person kisses the palm of his hand and bows before him with his forehead touching the ground. The sheikh hands him the *zarp*, which the dervish kisses and then whirls, while dancing, so that the chains stand out horizontally. He then kneels down and inserts it. I have witnessed the *zarp* being inserted through the inside of one cheek with the point emerging on the outside, and through the outside of the right cheek with the point penetrating both cheeks and emerging through the left. I have also seen it inserted behind the collarbone, into the eye socket, and through clothing so that it penetrated the flesh around the waist. The devotee rises, walks around the room for a few minutes, removes the *zarp*, kisses it and hands it back to the sheikh. There is normally no bleeding. Occasionally, the sheikh touches the cheek of the dervish as if to heal a wound. *Ashik*s and young boys may ask the sheikh to insert a *t'g* through one or both cheeks. 'They come to me like sacrificial lambs', Erol Baba used to say tenderly. In the meantime, the dervishes continue to chant. The *kiyami* and *devrani* ritual is sometimes concluded by another form of *devran* in which all taking part in the *zikr* go around the room, holding hands.

All are seated for the conclusion of the ceremony. A dervish recites from the Koran, Amdi sings one or more *ilahis*, and the leader says a prayer to a background chorus of *amin* ('amen') *Allah-amin-Allah*. They also recite the *ruh-i pak* sequence to which Marsol refers.[25] This is followed by a prolonged prayer session in which each participant in turn proposes a *Fatiha* to be read, for God, for the soul (*ruhiçin*) of the Prophet, for one or more of the saints, or for all men of God (*erenler*). The sheikh or his *vekil* recites a long standard list of those for whose souls a *Fatiha* is intended: Hasan, Husayn, the twelve Imams, the 'twelve *tarikat* founders', Sersem Ali Baba, the founder of the Bektashi *tekke* in Tetovo, Haydar Baba and others.[26] The *zikr* ends with a prostration by the entire *halka*, saying *hu-hu-hu* as they did at the beginning. Finally, they all stand in rows behind the sheikh facing in the direction of Haznadar Baba's tomb and pray briefly for Haznadar and Pir Ahmad ar-Rifa'i.

Once the ceremony is over, the participants recline against the walls of the *zikr* room for *muabet* (Arabic: *muhabba*, 'showing regard or friendship, loving'), also called *suhbet* (Arabic: *suhba*, 'friendship, companionship') or *munakasha* (Arabic: *munaqasha*, 'discussion' or 'dispute'), a conversation about matters of religion, ethics, good manners (*edep*) or simply the mundane affairs of the *tekke*.

A New Sheikh

In July or August of 2005, Amdi had a dream in which Haznadar Baba[27] told him that Sheikh Erol was soon to join the ranks of the saints, and would be buried in the *turbe*. Amdi relayed this information to the sheikh, who said he knew. Amdi then asked whether after his death the sheikh would be willing to help him, and Erol Baba told him to just come and pray. So Amdi proceeded to prepare the future saint's *kubur*. Somewhat later, during the summer holidays, Arben had a dream in which a *zikr* was opened by Baba Erol but closed by his son Murtezan.

At the beginning of September, Erol Baba was admitted to the hospital, where he died on the 16th. The next day he was buried in the *turbe*. Forty days after his death a ceremony was conducted at the Skopje *tekke* in which Sheikh Mehdi of the Rifa'i *tekke* in Orahovac also participated, with twenty of his dervishes. *Ilahi*s were sung, the *taj*, the *jubbe* and the *kemer* of the deceased were placed on the tomb, and a *zikr* was performed in the *semaana*.

It was easy to decide that Murtezan would be the next sheikh. His brother Semi was not interested, and Murtezan had received an Islamic education at the *medrese*.

On March 22, 2006 Murtezan 'took the hand' from Sheikh Mehdi at Orahovac. The ceremony was made to coincide with the celebration of Sultan Nevruz, the birthday of Ali, and the *semaana* was filled to capacity with hundreds of dervishes. Many women watched the proceedings from the gallery. After an hour of *ilahi* singing, twelve candles were lit. Murtezan prayed ten *rak'as*, and then was taken by the *rehber*[28] and two *bayraktar*s to sit in front of Sheikh Mehdi. Sheikh Mehdi was sitting on his *post*, in the *semaana's mihrab*, the niche which is directed towards Mecca. Behind the *mihrab* is the tomb of Mehdi's father, Sheikh Baki. Next to Sheikh Mehdi sat the sheikh who had given him the hand, Sheikh Mazhar from Gjakova/Djakovica. The congregation intoned *la ilaha illa 'llah* and kept it up during the next half hour. A large black cloth was thrown over Sheikh Mehdi and Murtezan, so that the Secret, the *sirr*, could be communicated in private. Next, Murtezan, a sheikh now, received the *taj*, the *jubbe* and the *kemer* which he was henceforth entitled to wear. He kept his given name.

The session, which lasted a full three hours in all, was concluded by a massive *zikr* of more than an hour, with a deafening chanting of *esma*s accompanied by percussion on hand-held *kudum*s and *def*s. During the *zikr*, Amdi, who had accompanied Murtezan to Orahovac along with Yashar and Arben, sang one of his favourite *ilahi*s in Turkish.

Sheikh Mazhar and Sheikh Mehdi turned around in a *devran*, holding hands. Before leaving the *tekke* the visitors were given a generous lunch in the *semaana*. After our return to Skopje, Arben and Amdi went straight to the *turbe* to report to Haznadar Baba and Erol Baba. Three days later Sheikh Mehdi came to Skopje with his dervishes 'to put Sheikh Murtezan on his *post*' in a ceremony which was again combined with the local Nevruz celebration.

Sheikh Mehdi has promised to coach Murtezan for a while. The latter never involved himself much in the affairs of the *tekke* before, but he is treated with due respect by his dervishes, many of whom know the ritual better than he does. He has a job at the Ministry of Defence, so he cannot open the *turbe* to visitors during the day like Baba Erol used to do. This task is now being assumed by the *Shehana*, Erol Baba's widow Naime.

There are five Rifa'i *tekke*s in Kosovo and Macedonia. The sheikhs in Prizren, Gjakova/Djakovica, Rahovec/Orahovac and Skopje are now in 2006 forty, thirty-four, thirty and twenty-four years of age, respectively. The confirmation of the fifth sheikh, due to head the Mitrovica *tekke*, may occur sometime soon, again at Orahovac.

The 'taking the hand' ritual for a new sheikh is a rare event, and in view of the young age of the present generation of sheikhs it may well become extremely rare for decades to come. These young Rifa'i sheikhs may last for decades and as they settle in they will provide stability and stimulate the further growth of their communities. They combine their fervour in the rituals with great tolerance towards other forms of worship.

In perpetuating their ancient traditions they will continue to make a specific and valuable contribution to the multi-faceted culture of the Balkans.

C. Sheikh Murtezan standing beside the tomb of Haznadar Baba

Endnotes

1) Annemarie Schimmel, *Mystical Dimensions of Islam*, The University of North Carolina Press, 1975.

2) For Centuries They Waited, For Years They Celebrated. *Ilahis* and *zikr* ceremony. Skopje Rifai Dervishes. PAN Records no. 2110, www.panrecords.nl.

3) I shall follow the Turkish terminology derived from the Persian, as it is used in the Balkans, *tarikat, hakikat,* etc. instead of the Arabic *tariqa, haqiqa*. For the sake of visual simplicity I am omitting the finesses of Arabic transliteration such as diacritical dots distinguishing between various d's, h's, s's, t's and z's and strokes indicating long vowels.

4) The Turkish mystic Yunus Emre, who died around 1320, may be the most important folk poet in Islamic literature, and he is still widely known and quoted, including in one of the *ilahi*s sung in Skopje.

5) Without describing himself as a Shiite, Sheikh Erol distinguished between 'Sufis' and 'Sunnis,' the latter referring to the orthodox Muslims and their leaders, or *hodža*s.

6) In Persian, *sama'*, literally (Arabic) 'hearing,' denotes a spiritual concert or ecstasy occasioned by hearing such music. A *sama'-khana* is a house or hall where this music is performed. In Macedonia, where there is a general tendency to drop the *h*, the word has become *semaana*, and refers either to the ceremonial *zikr* hall in the *tekke* or to a place outside the *tekke* where *zikr*s are organized led by a *vekil* authorized by the sheikh.

7) *Bog je jedan, a vjera ima na stotine.* (*Jutarnji List,* July 17, 2006, p.56: *Branitelji oboljeli od PTSP-a u pomoć pozvali derviše*). Sheikh Osmani is a Sufi healer based in Zagreb.

8) See John R. Walsh, *Yunus Emre, a 14th-Century Hymnodist* in Talat Halman (ed.), *Yunus Emre and His Mystical Poetry*, Indiana University Turkish Studies, 1984.

9) From a conversation with Father Cordignano, see Alexandre Popović, *Un Ordre de Derviches en Terre d'Europe*, Lausanne, 1993, p. 50. See also H.T. Norris, *Islam in the Balkans*, The University of South Carolina Press.

10) The dervish orders generally trace their spiritual ancestry back to Ali, but without elevating him to the position he occupies in the doctrine of the Macedonian Rifa'is.

11) In Serbian/Bosnian: *'Muhamed je Alija, Ali-Muhamed, Alija je Muhamed, Ali-Muhamed, Allah! Alija je Muhamed, Ali-Muhamed.'*

12) *Allahumme! Salli 'ala sayyidina Muhammadin wa-'ala ..* (pause) *.. 'Ali-Muhammad!*

13) *'Oniki imam oniki piran ruhiçin.'* The number of twelve for the main *tarikat*s and their founders looks artificial and based on an analogy with the twelve Imams.

14) Q : *'Jesu li derviši suniti ili šijiti?'*
    A : *'Mi smo sunije po mezhebu, ali vjerujemo isto što i šijiti.'*
    (*Nedjeljna Dalmacija*, August 12, 1990, p. 25).

15) respectively, *ehli sheriat, ehli tarikat, ehli marifet* and *ehli hakikat*.

16) *ente lehadi, ente lehak, leyse lehadi illa hu* (Arabic: *anta 'l-hadi, anta 'l-haqq, laysa 'l-hadi illa huwa*, i.e., You are the Guide, You are the Truth, no-one is the Guide but He.)

17) This technique is mentioned in Gl. Elezović, *Derviški Redovi Muslimanski, Tekije u Skoplju*, Skopje, 1925.

18) Liliana Mašulović-Marsol describes in detail the *zikr* she witnessed in the *tekke*'s *semaana* on 3 October, 1981 in *Les Rifa'is de Skopje, structure et impact*, Istanbul, 1992.

19) L. Gardet, *Dhikr* in Encyclopaedia of Islam.

20) The Mevlevis also use a *kudum*, which however is beaten with two small sticks.

21) A very similar situation prevails at an annual celebration called the *nadar* in the Sukabumi region in West Java, during which the participants read the Hikayat Syekh Abdulkadir Jaelani, a chronicle of the life of the Sufi Pir Abdul Qadir al-Jilani (Endo Suanda, *Reading Together*, in *Prince Claus Fund Journal* no. 12, April 2006). The reading is done partly in Sundanese, the regional language, and partly in Javanese, which 90% of the participants don't understand. This doesn't present a problem. As Mr Suanda says, 'The Javanese language ... is not mainly to be understood intellectually, but in a

different fashion, because it has spiritual and historical meaning ... The words are not meant as 'language' but rather as sounds; words become something organic, something to feed body and soul ... They (i.e., the participants) seem to be creating, practicing and enjoying an atmosphere together. Indeed, the atmosphere can't be heard or seen, but must be felt. The feeling is that of being one and not separated ... Spiritual energy or atmosphere is not created by clarity, but rather by the absence of it.'

22) *astaghfiru 'llah.*

23) *la ilaha illa 'llah, Muhammadun rasulu 'llah.*

24) i.e., '(Oh!) Everlasting One, Truth, God, Living One!' These are four of Allah's ninety-nine 'most beautiful names' (Arabic: *al-asma' al-husna*).

25) The leader sings: '(Oh!) pure spirit' (*ruh-i pak*) and the group replies: 'Bless Muhammad' (*salli 'ala Muhammad*); the leader then sings, 'pure body' (*jism-i pak*)! to which the group reiterates the first reply, followed by 'pure name' (*ism-i pak*)! again with the same reply. They end by singing twice: '*Allahu ekber, Allahu ekber, la ilaha illa 'llah*: God is greater, God is greater, there is no god but God.'

26) After each prayer they repeat the formula quoted in endnote 12.

27) I asked Amdi how he recognized Haznadar Baba when he saw him in a dream. Amdi replied that all dervishes knew what Haznadar Baba looked like: tall, and dressed in black. Amdi had once seen him praying in the *semaana*.

28) Murtezan was the third sheikh assisted by this *rehber*, after his father Erol in 1988 and, not long ago, Sheikh Mehdi.

1. The Rifa'i *tekke* in Skopje, seen from the Sheikh's private garden. The three small windows on the right belong to the *zikr* room; the larger windows are those of the guest room. The *turbe* with the holy tombs would be further to the left.

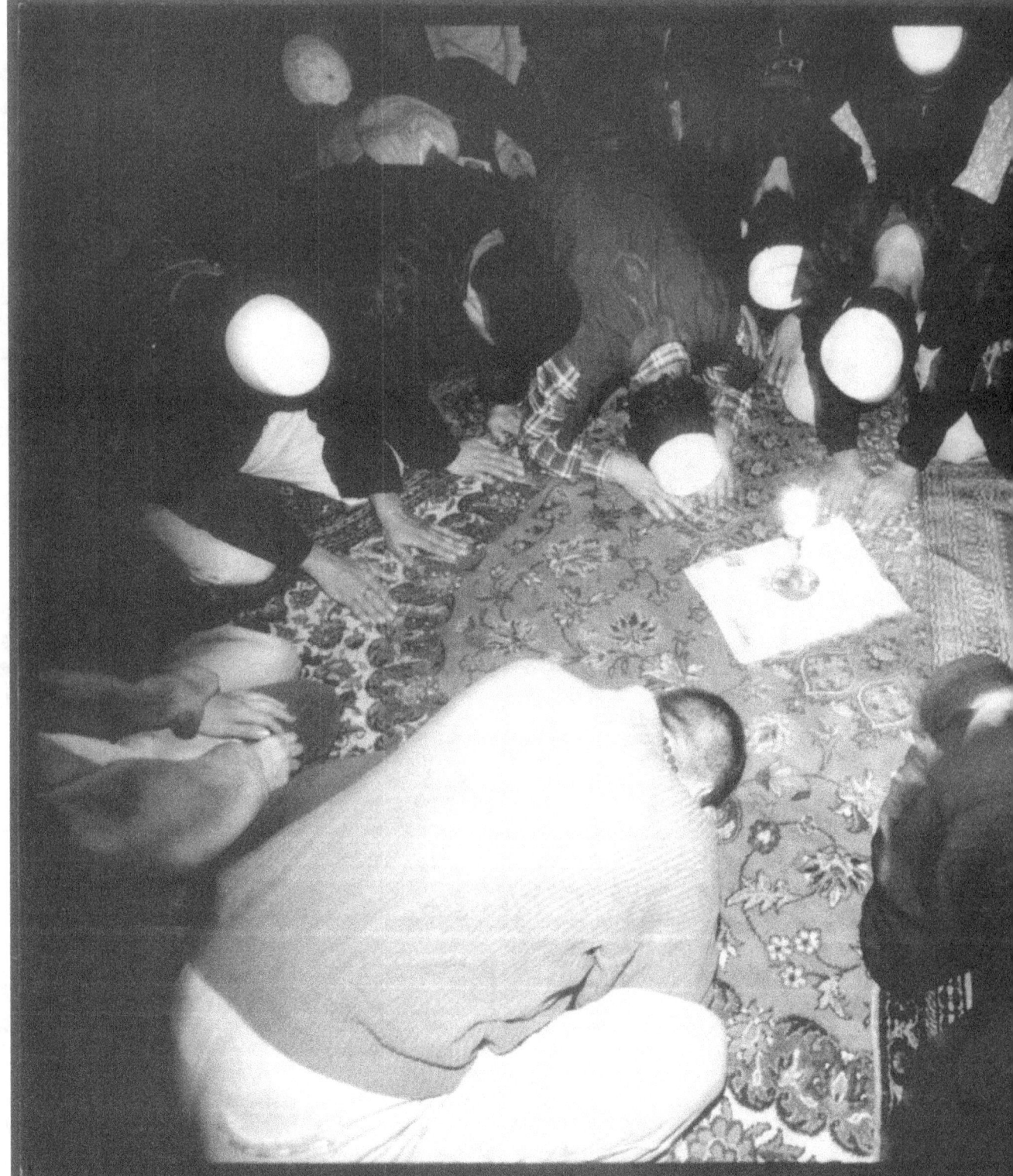

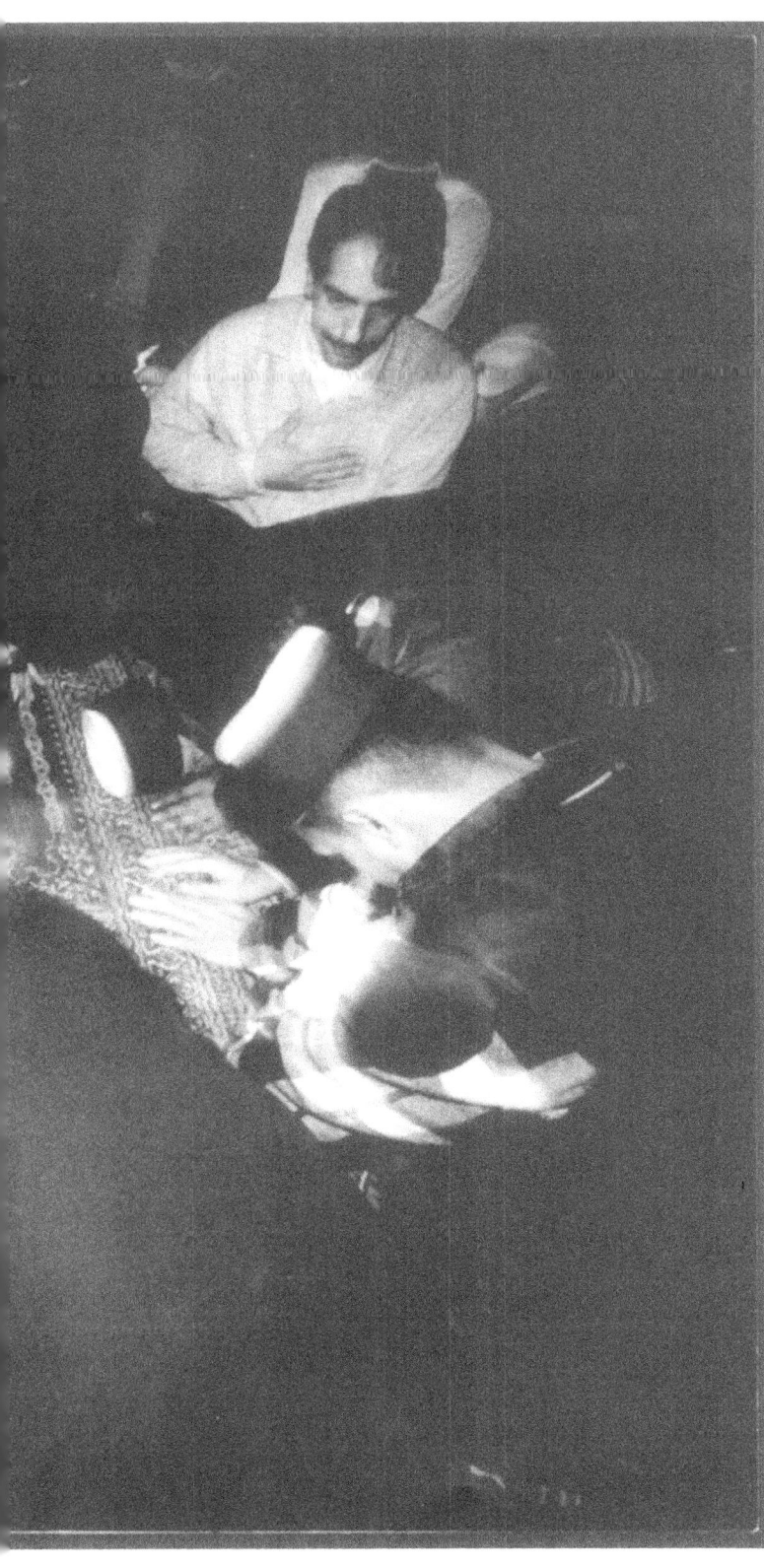

2. Starting the *zikr* with a prostration and the expression of sincerity.

3-6. Safet, Adem, Kerim, Amdi, Arben and some young boys at the sitting stage of the *zikr*.

4

7-8. *Ashik*s beating their *kudum*s. These were among my first photos at the *tekke*. Some of those present, like Amdi and Adem, subsequently became dervishes and were then allowed to wear the distinctive clothing shown in other pictures.

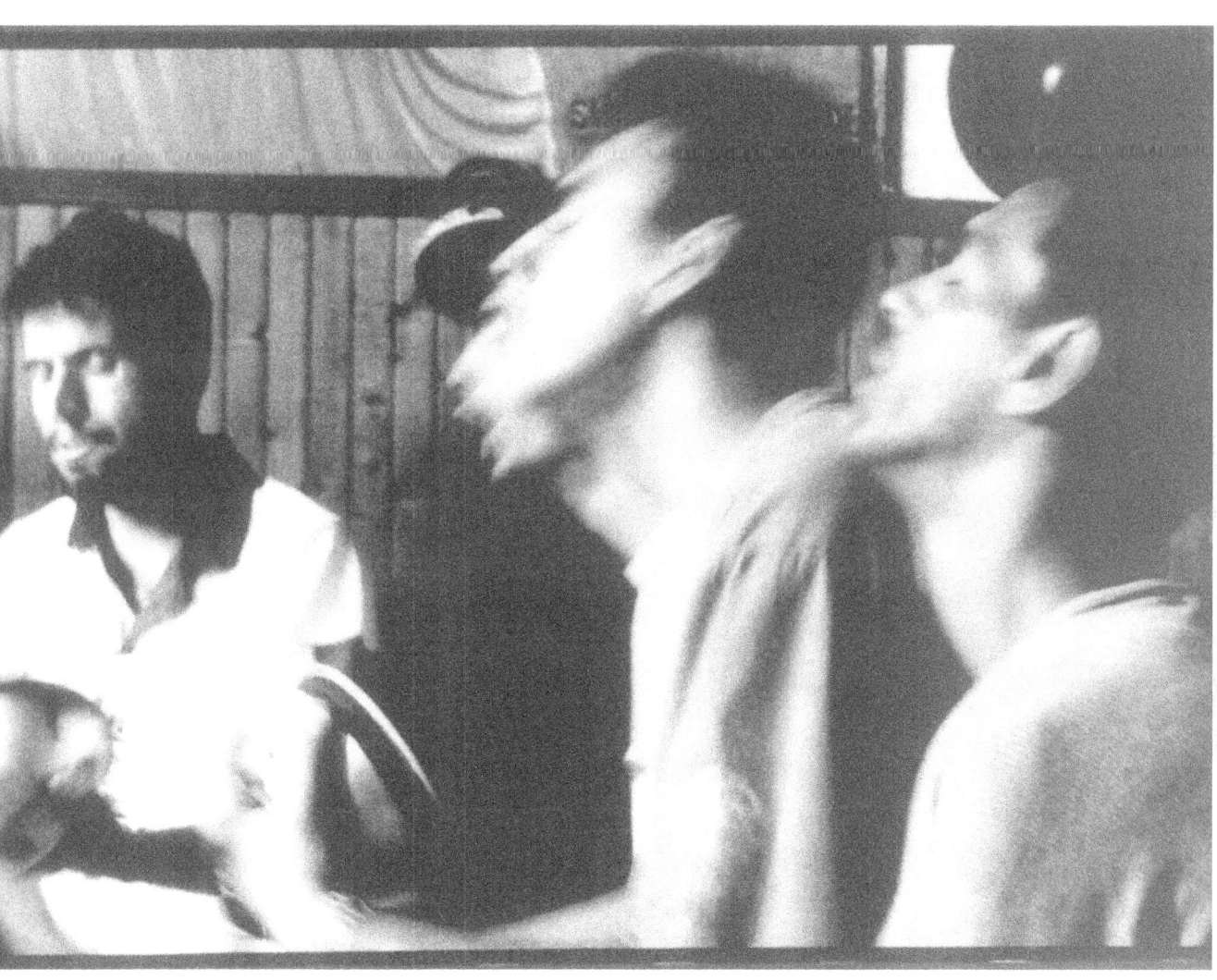

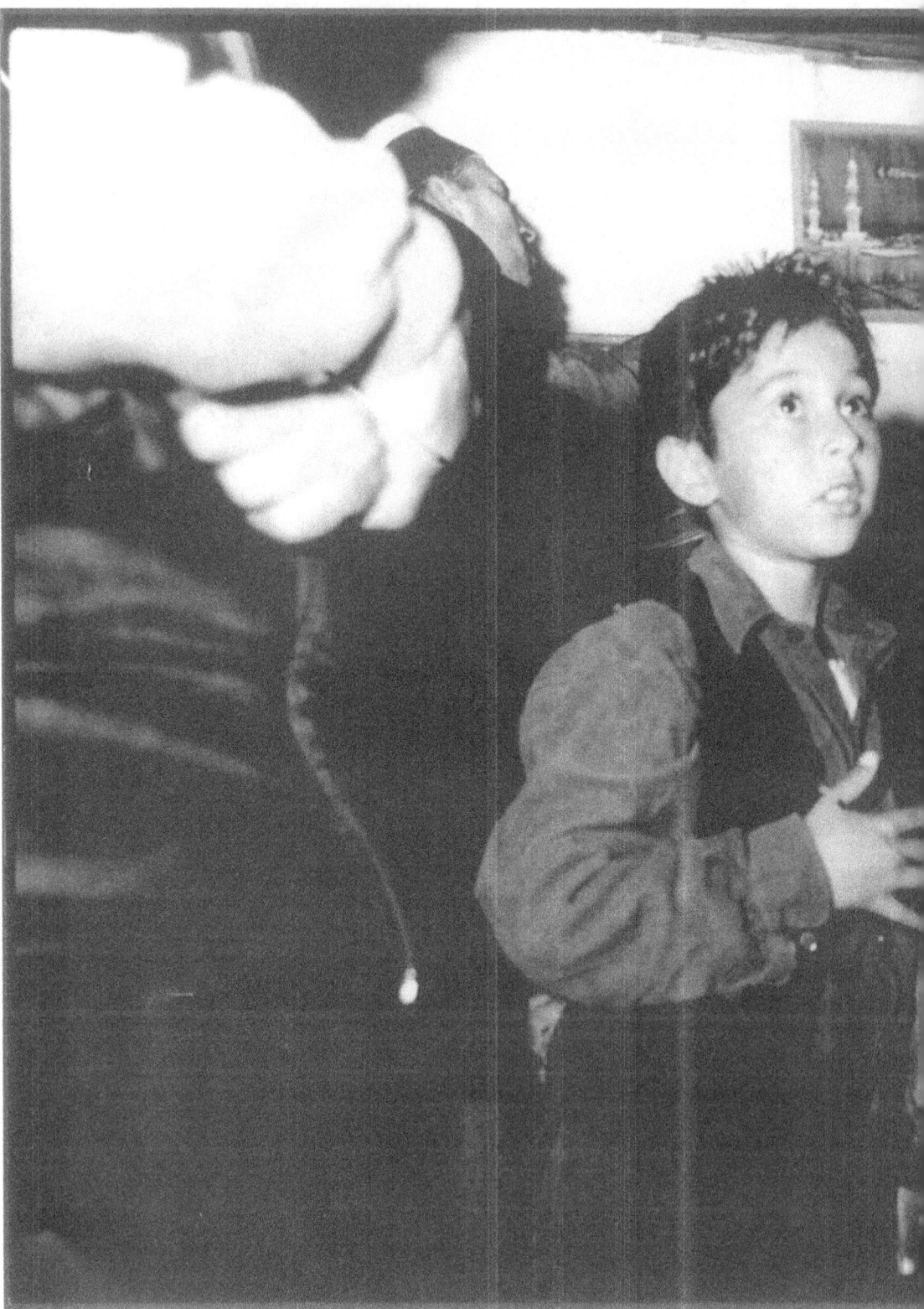

9. Beginning of the standing (*kiyami*) phase of the *zikr*.

10-11. Yashar leading the *zikr* as *vekil-zakirbashi*, using the *zil*.

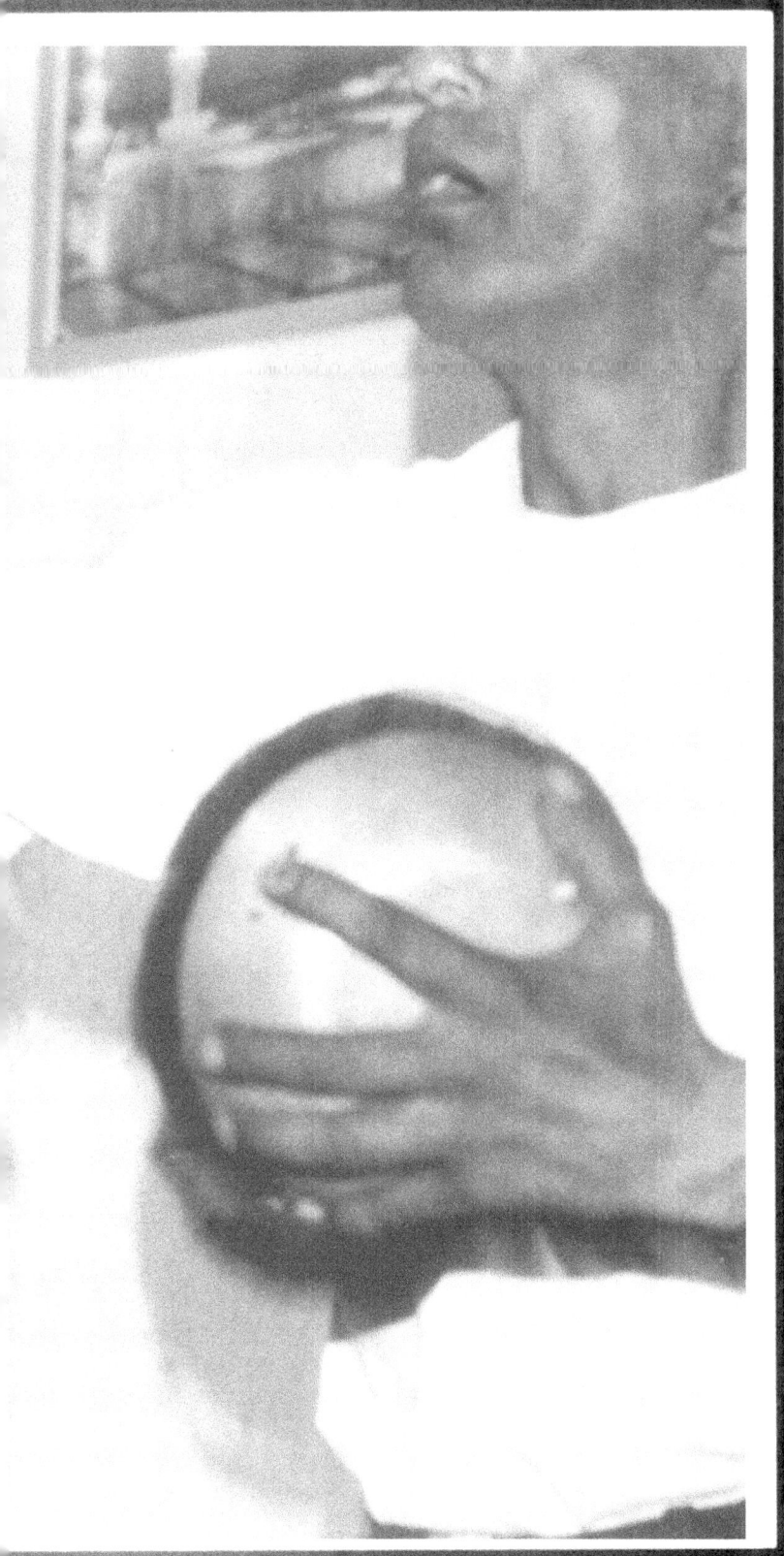

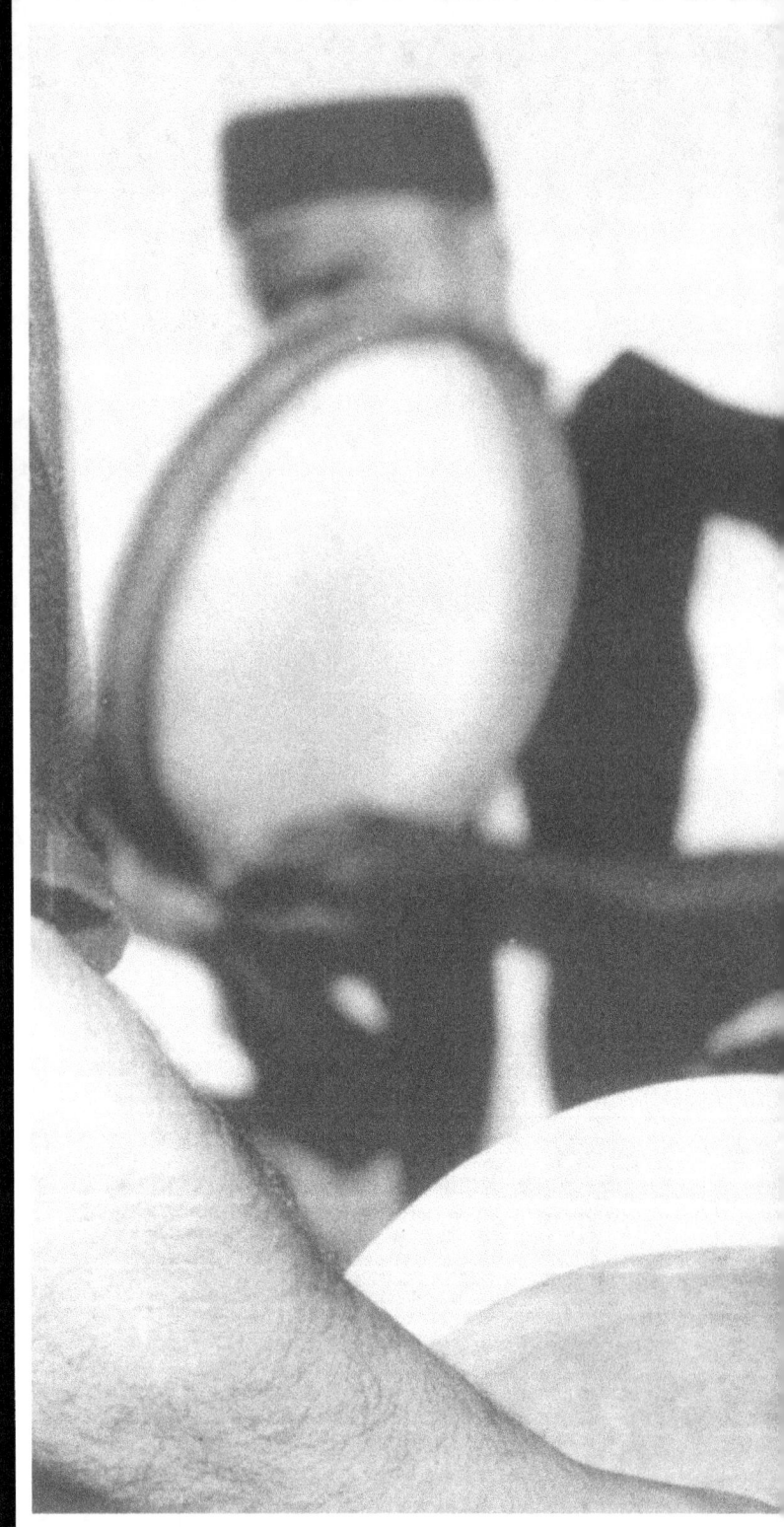

12. Dervishes singing and beating *def*s.

13. Buyami beating the *def*.

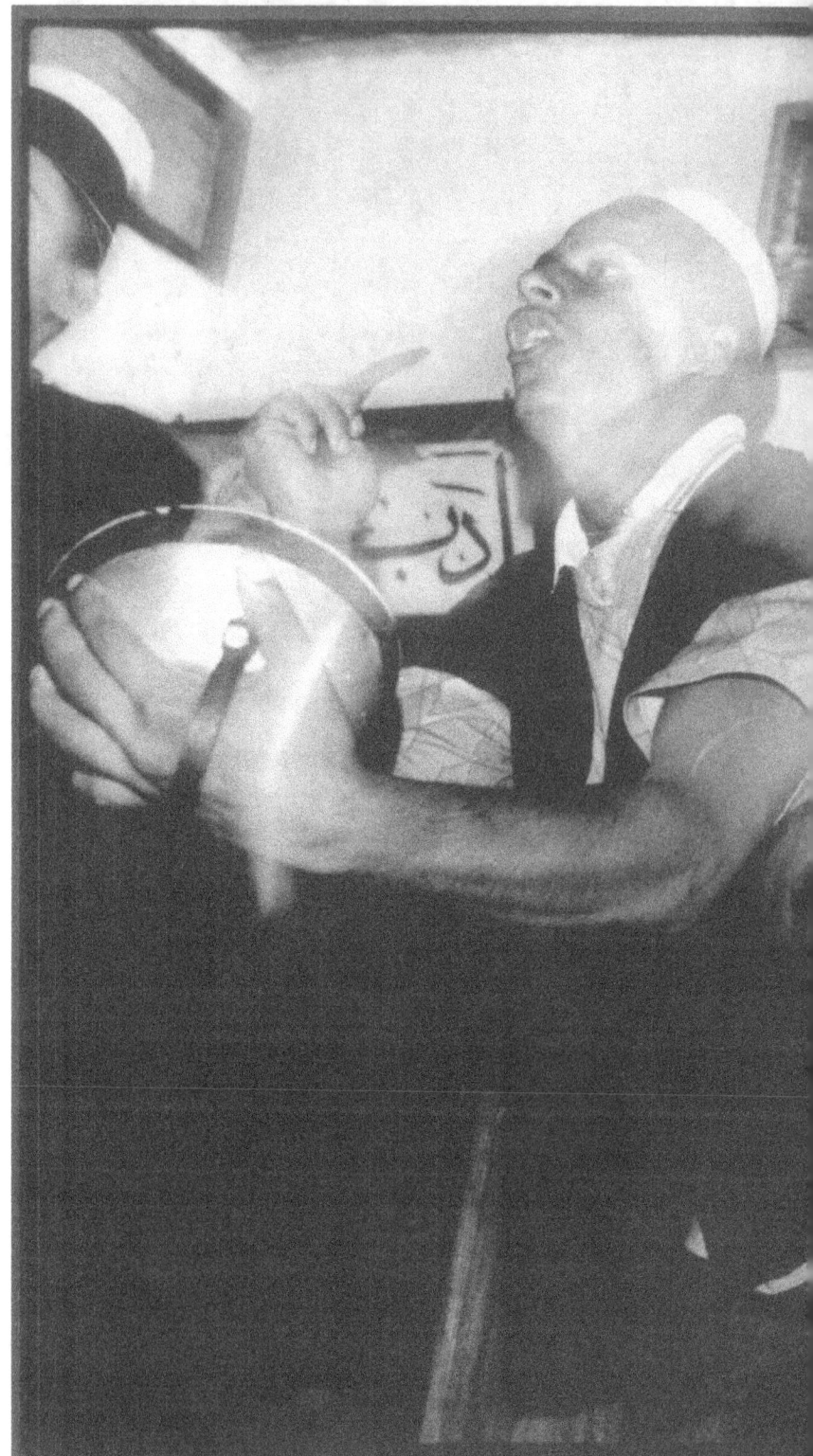
14. Dervishes beating *kudum*s.

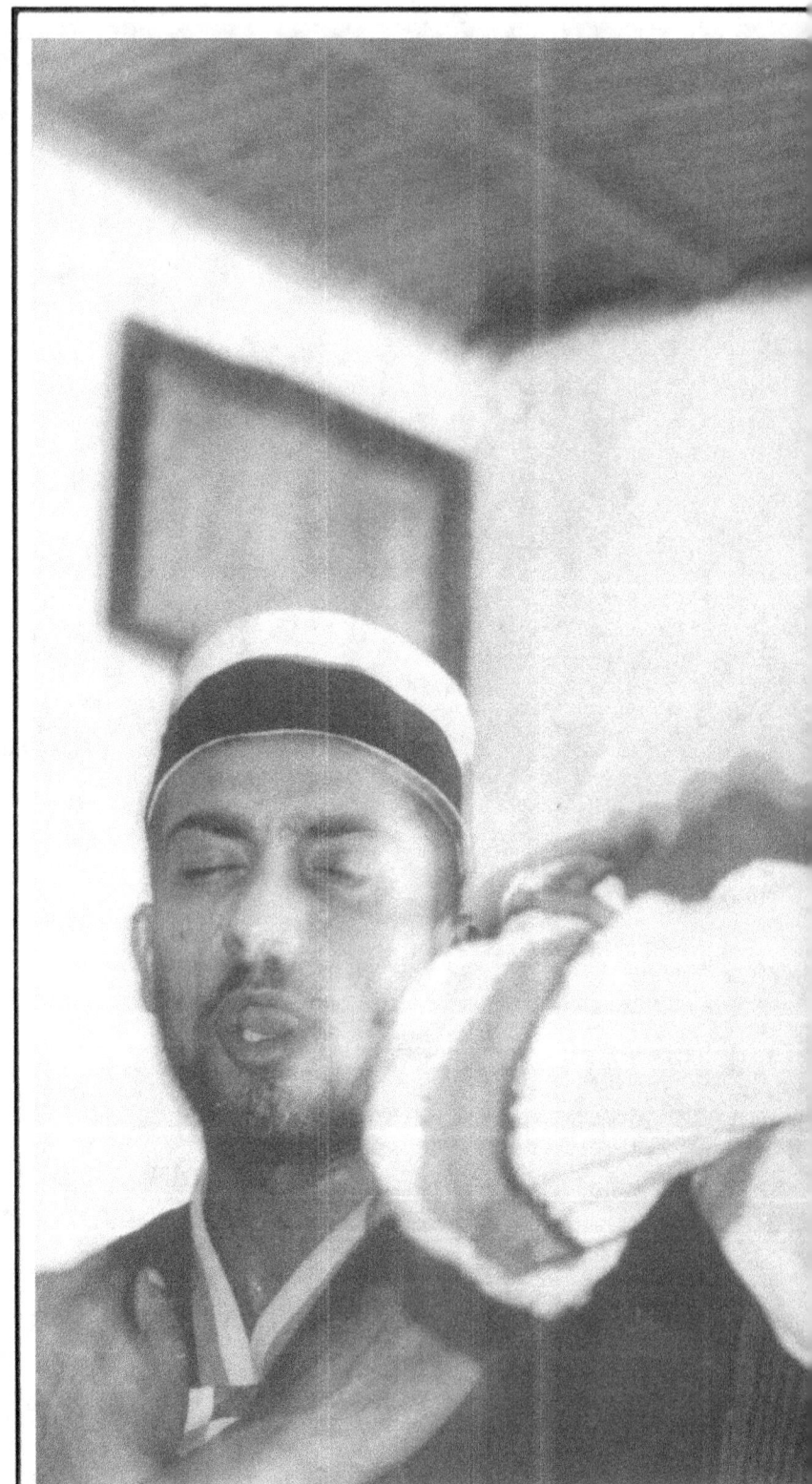

15. A moment of rapture.

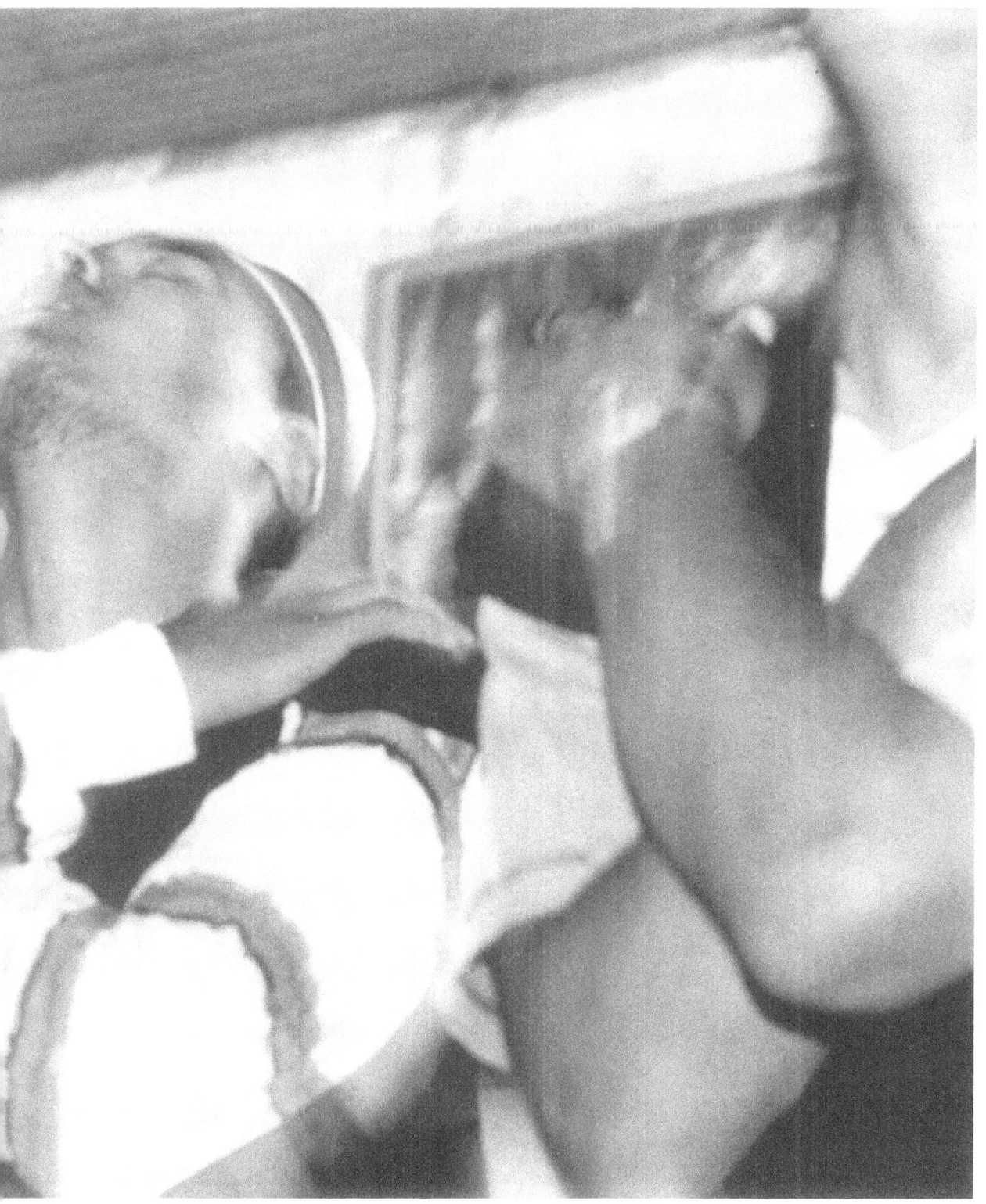

16. Beating the *zil* and *kudum*.

17. The visiting Sheikh Selim leading the *zikr*.

18-22. Children taking part in the *zikr*.

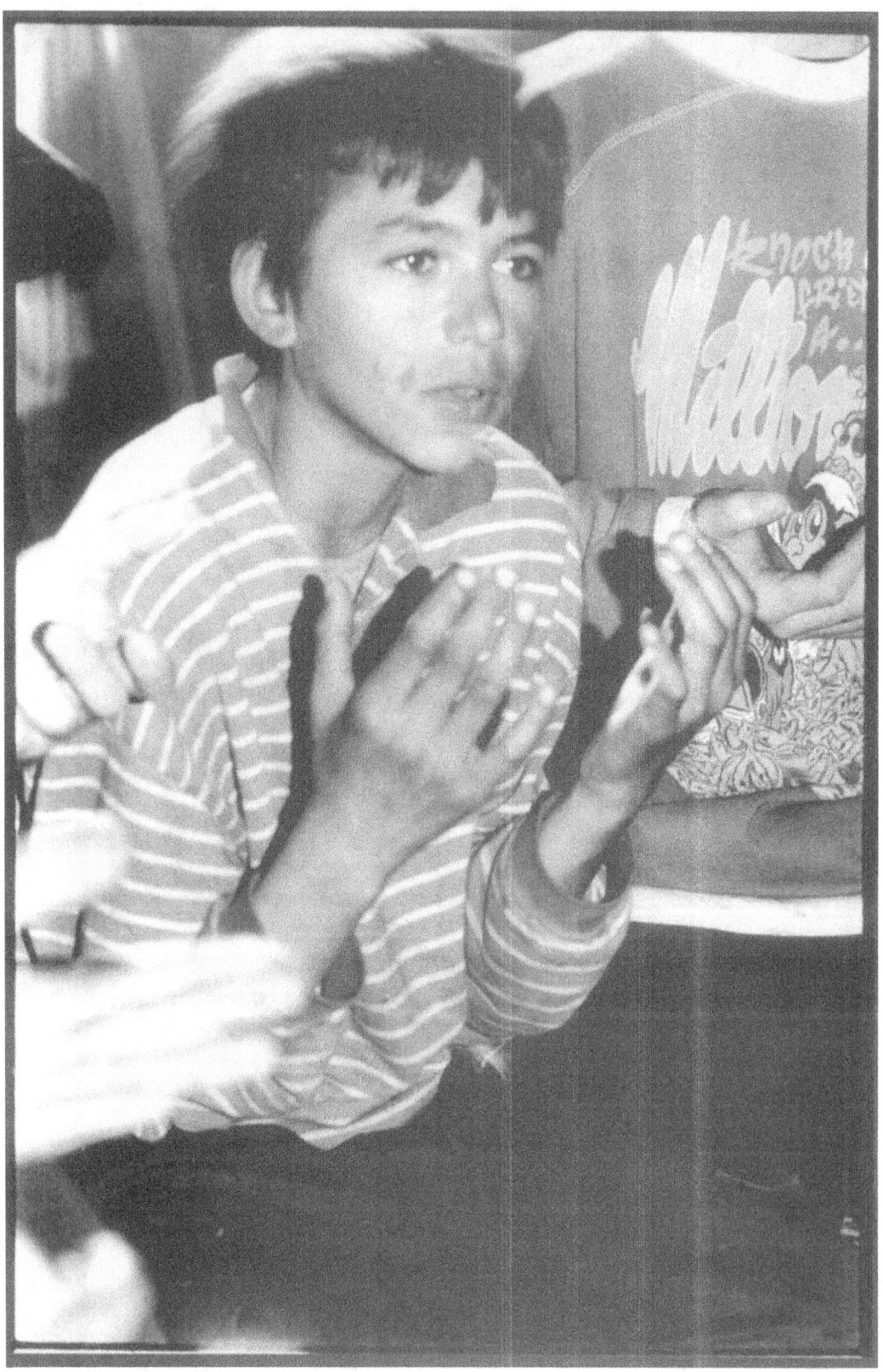

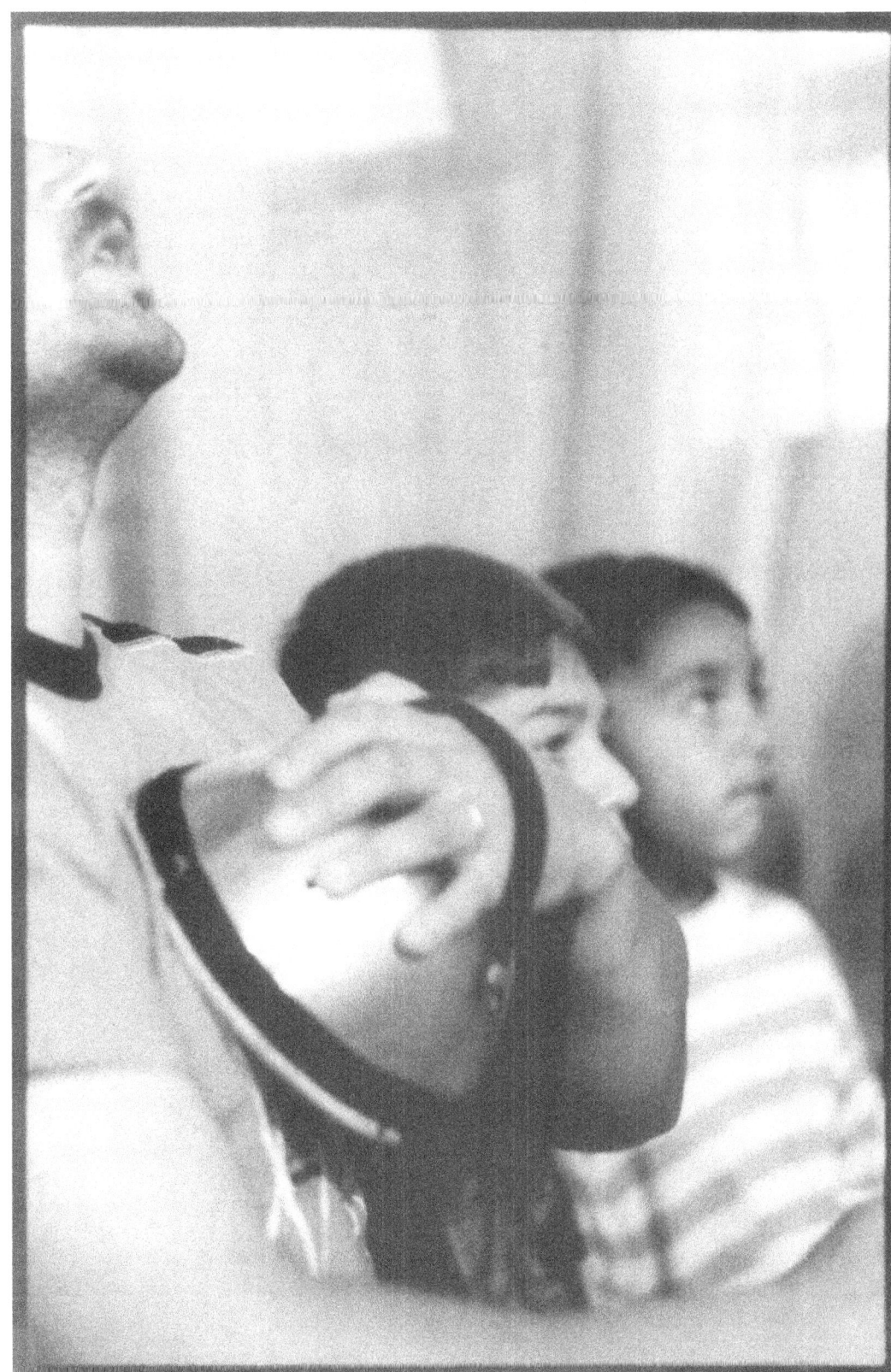

23. Baba Erol pierces a boy's cheek with a *t'g*.

24. The Sheikh pierced Buyami with a *zarp*.

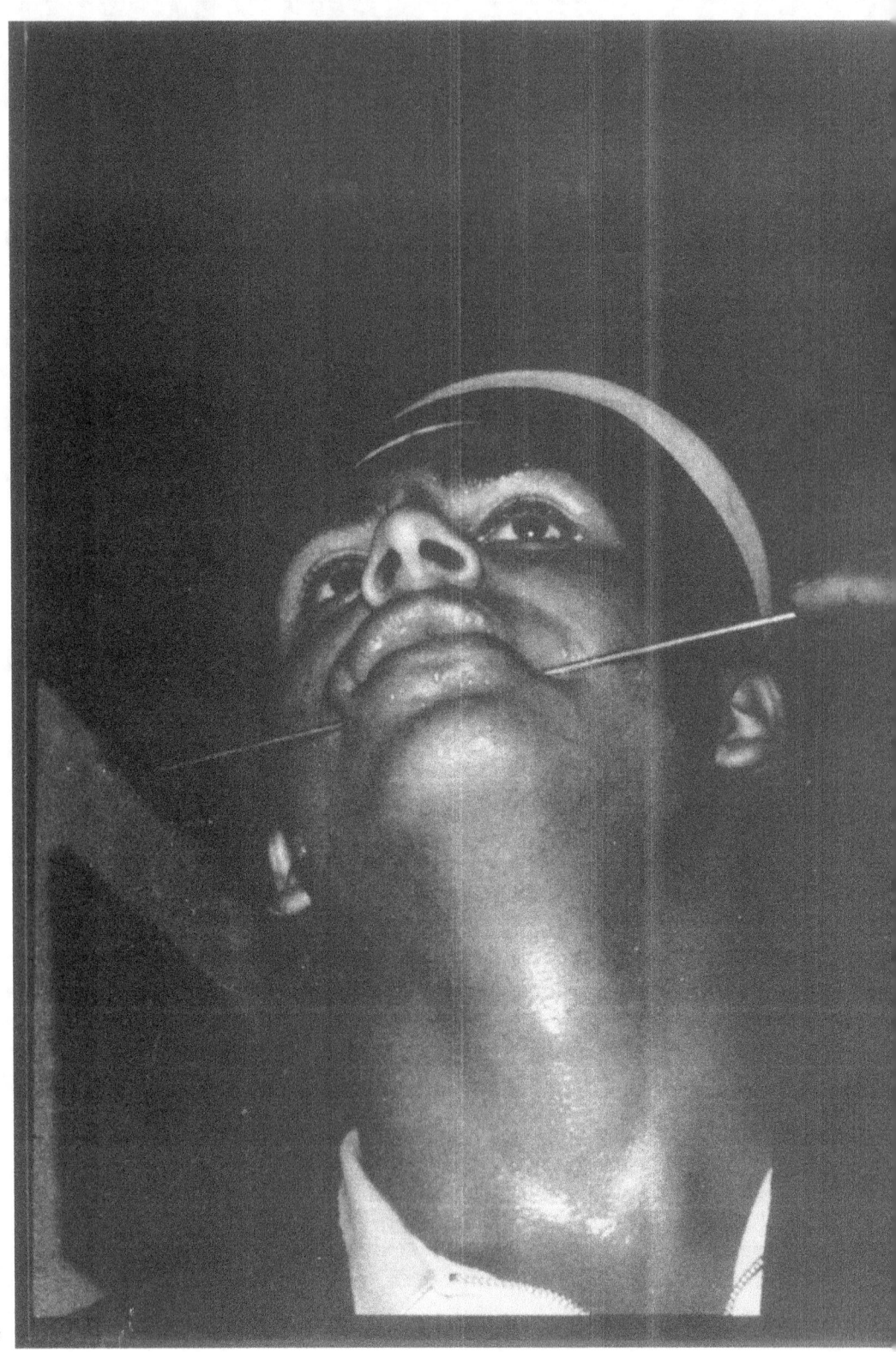

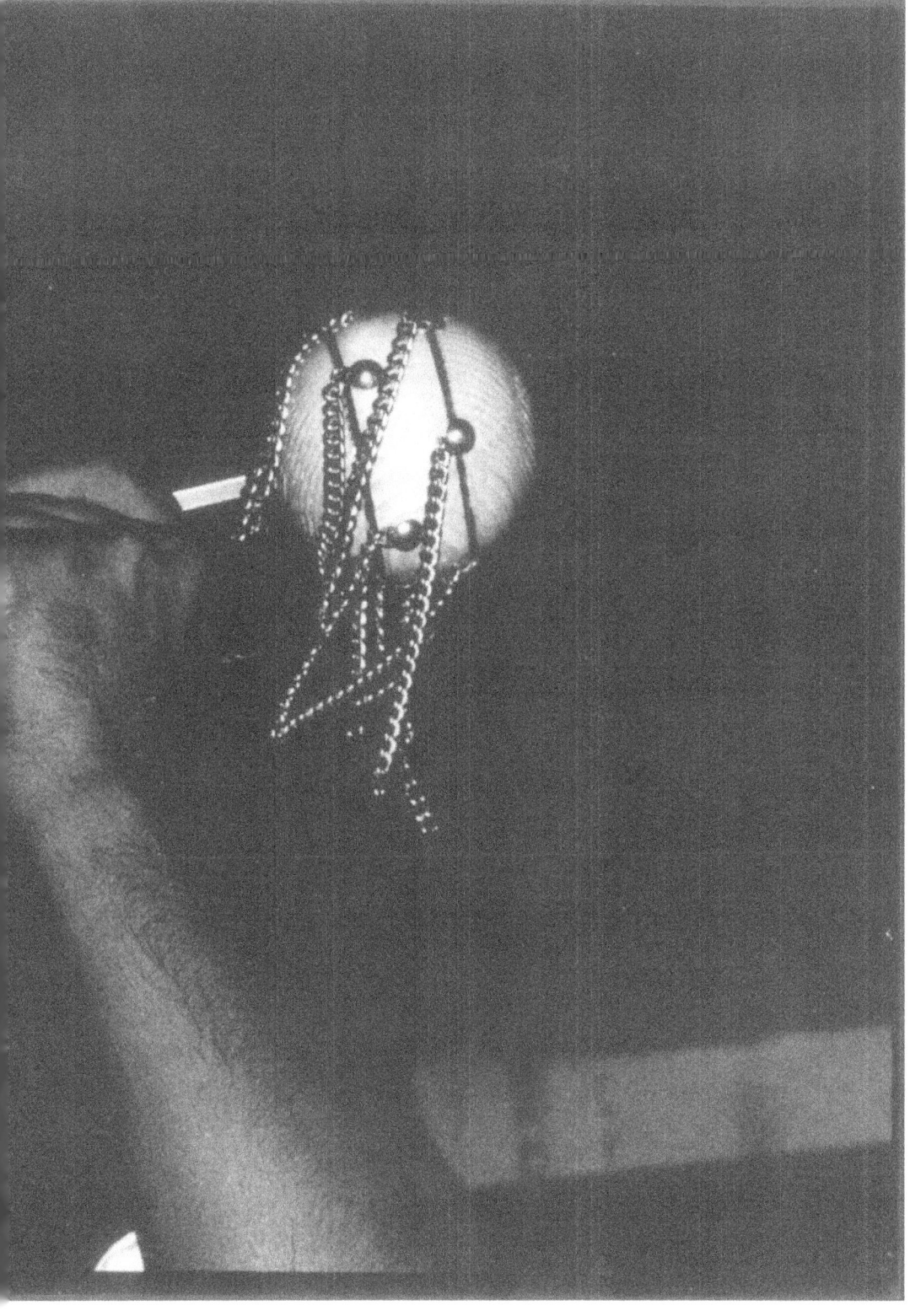

25. Yashar often pierced himself behind the collar bone.

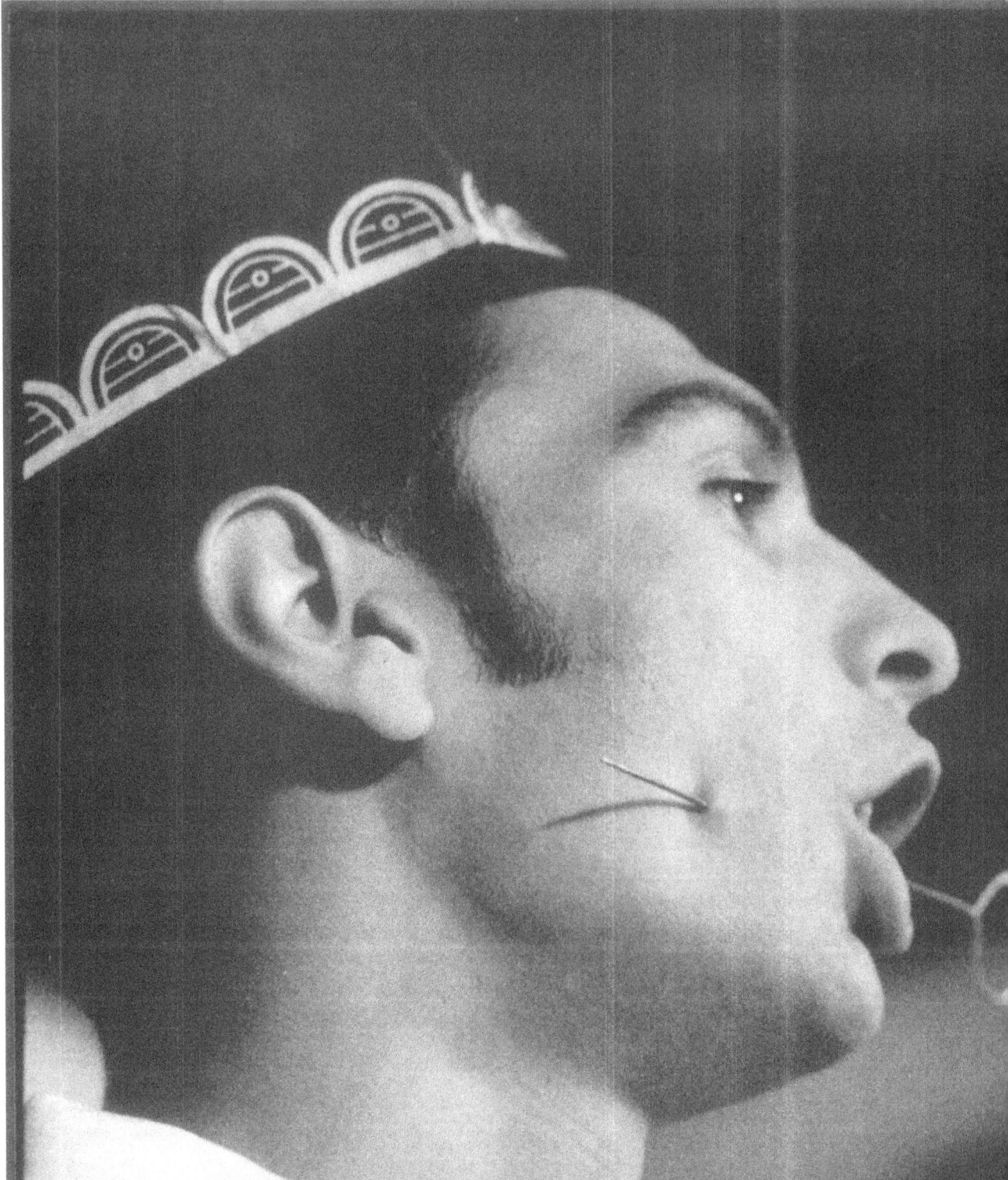

26. Adem with a *t'g*.

27. While those who have pierced themselves move around the room, the other participants continue the chanting.

28. The piercing is over, and some of the dervishes spin around slowly in an inner circle.

29-31. *Devran*s with two or four participants.

No. 29: Amdi

No. 30: Arben.

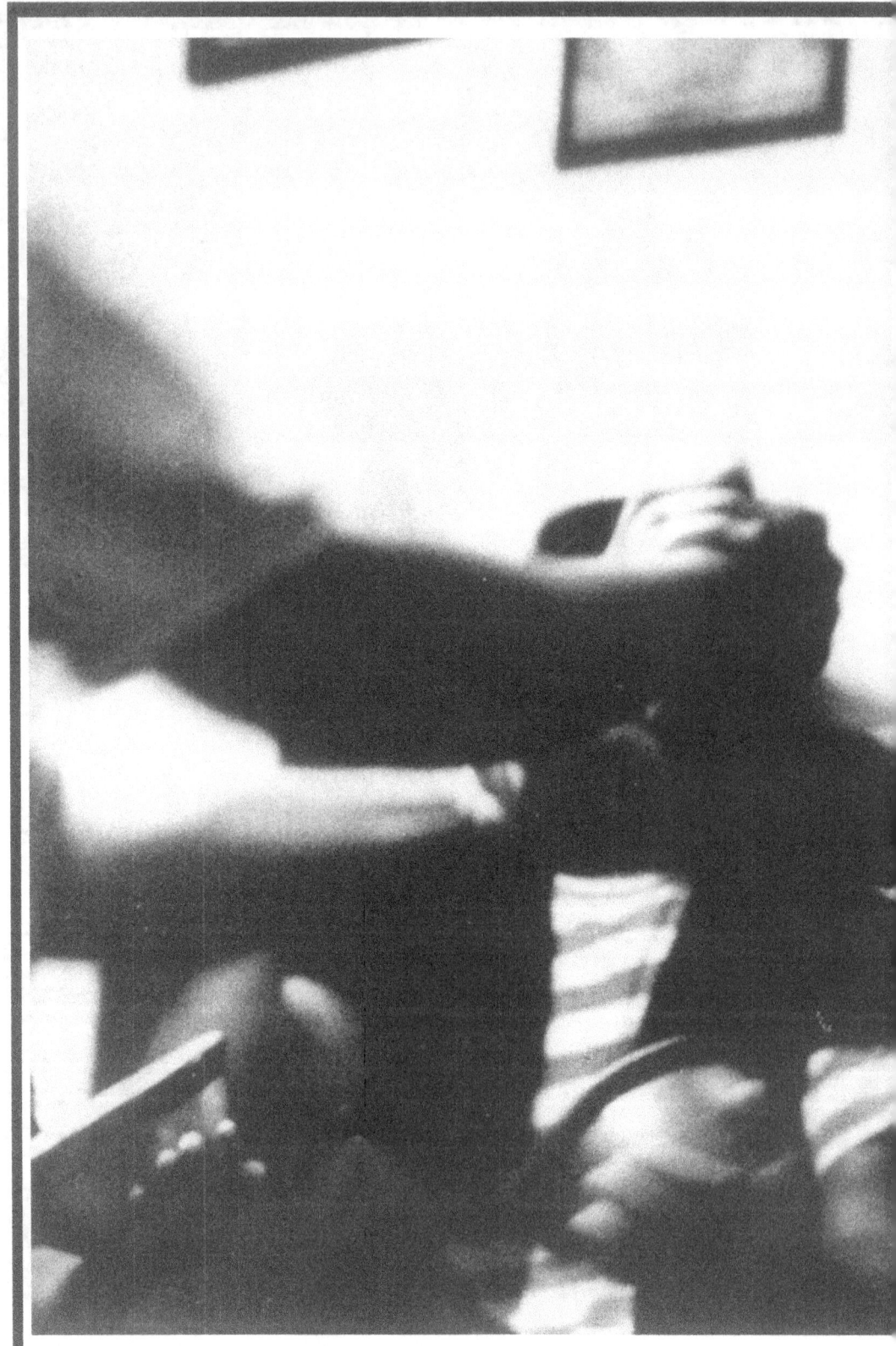

31

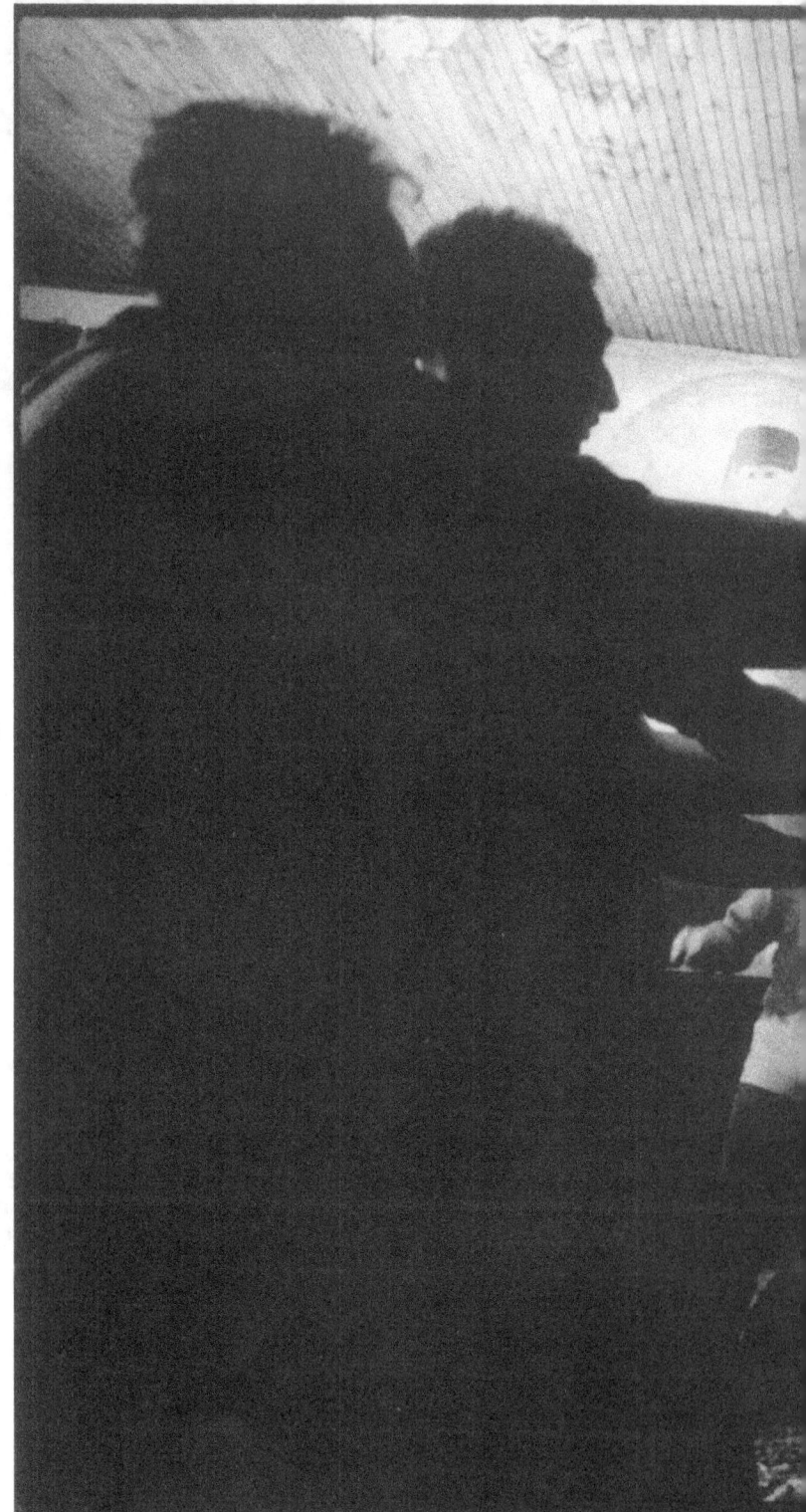

32-33. *Devran* at the end of the *zikr*.

33. Erol Baba and Amdi.

34. Closing the *zikr* with *'hu-hu-hu.'*

35-37. Inauguration ceremonies for dervishes.

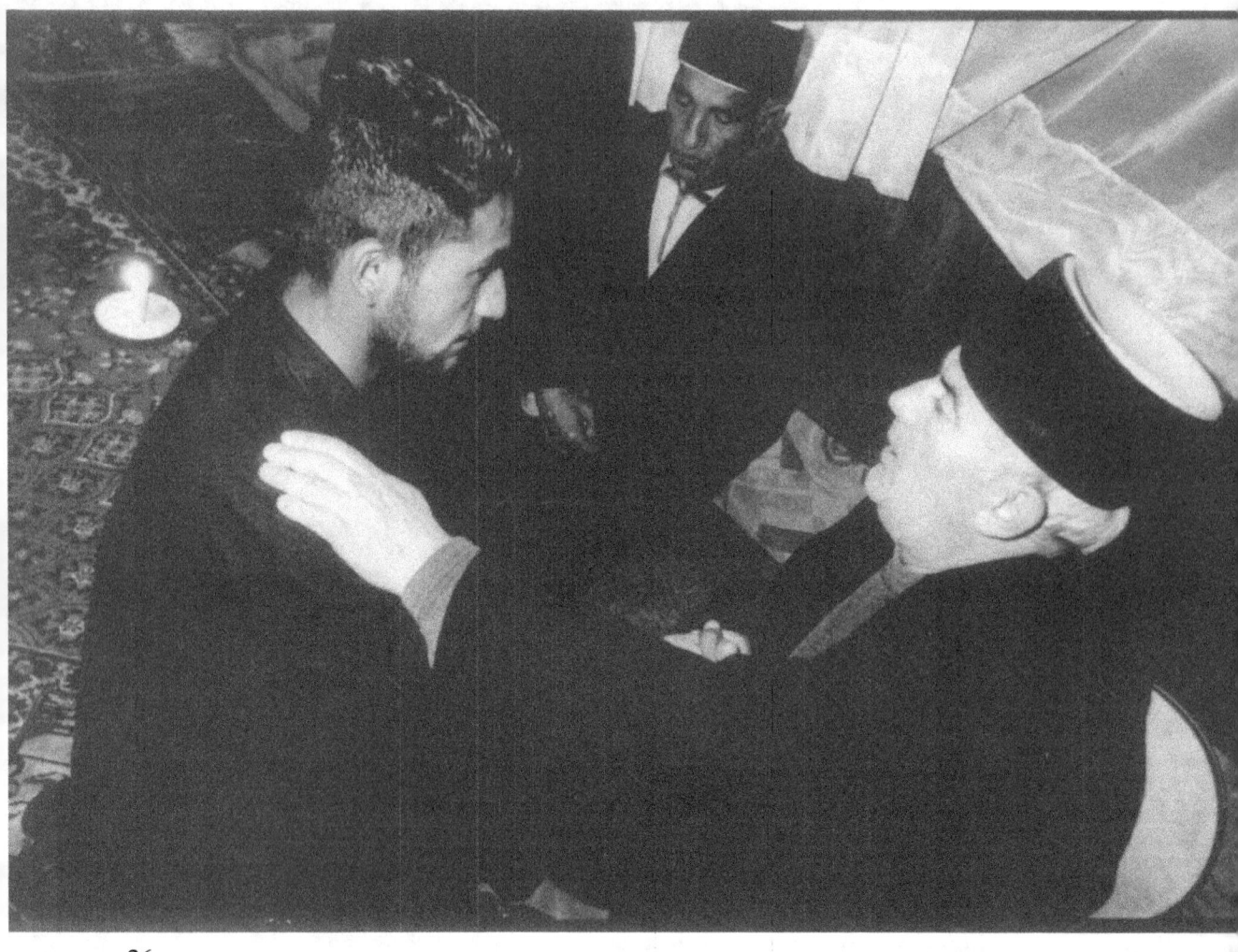

36

38. Inside the *turbe*. Erol Baba is seated with a 'patient' next to the tomb of Haznadar Baba. On the right, on the tomb of Erol Baba's father, Haydar Baba, are bottles of water absorbing *bereket*.

39. Erol Baba at the tomb of Haznadar Baba, after his operation. On the right are the antlers of a deer that came to sacrifice itself long ago, when a sheikh had no money for a *kurban*. The bags contain items left near the tombs for a few days for *bereket*.

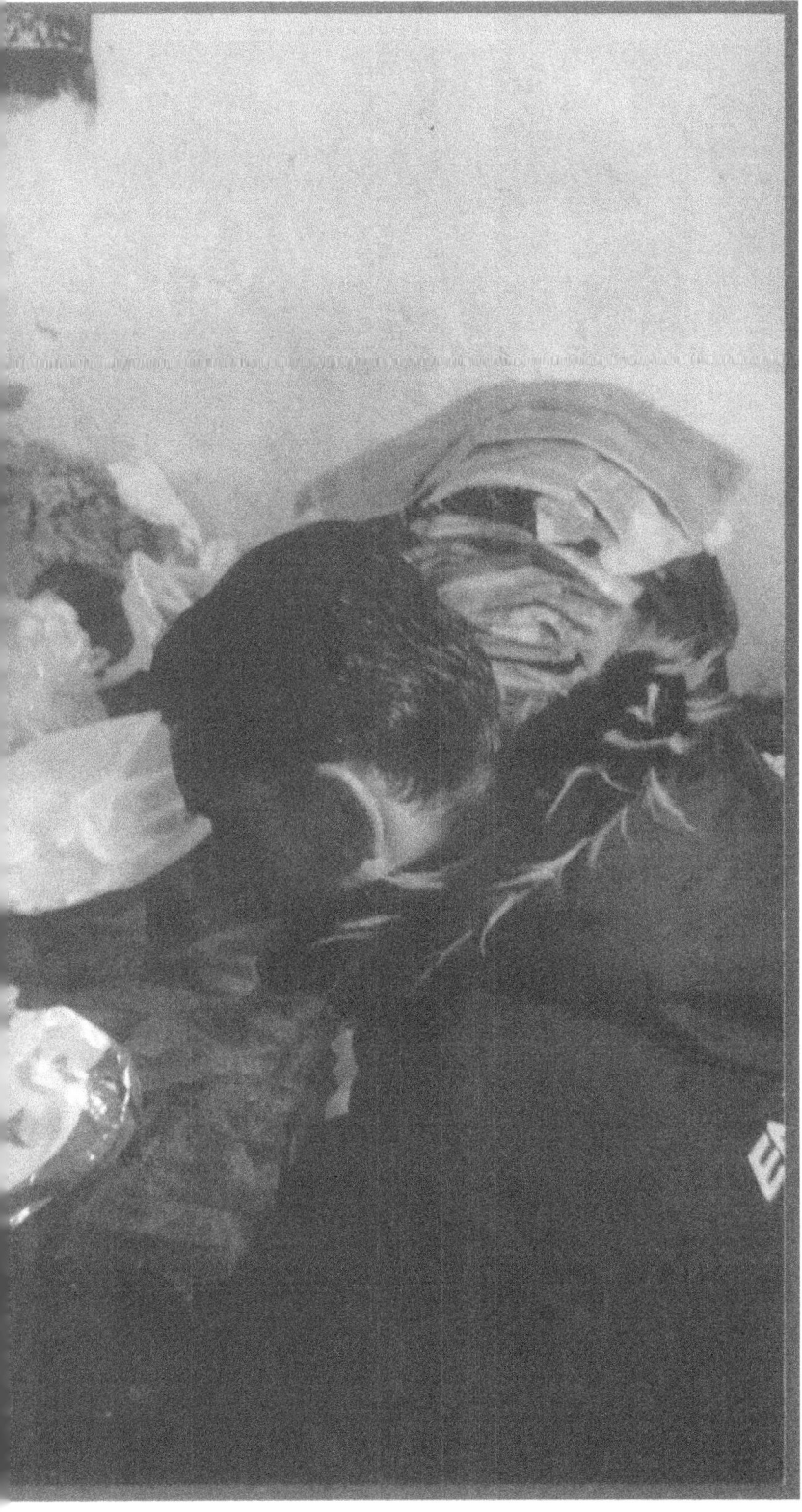

40. Erol Baba 'reading' for a boy brought in by his mother to help him find a wife.

The Baba's *taj* has twelve furrows. Around it there is a black turban; black being the distinctive colour of the Rifa'i order.

41. A Roma visitor accompanied by his wife making a pledge at the tomb of Haznadar Baba, with his hands on the headstone. Erol Baba dictates what he has to say.

42. Tombs of female relatives and wives of previous sheikhs, in the garden.

43. Tomb of a dervish in the garden.

44-49. The inauguration of Sheikh Murtezan at the *tekke* in Rahovec/Orahovac, Kosovo.

44. The *Rehber* and two *Bayraktar*s lead Murtezan to face Sheikh Mehdi.

45. Under a black cloth Sheikh Mehdi passes the Secret to Murtezan. The gentleman on the left is Mr Mustafa Orman, *vekil* at the Hadži Sinanova Tekija in Sarajevo, which belongs to the Qadiri *tarikat*. He attended as an important guest.

46-47. Murtezan receives the *taj*.

48. Sheikh Mazhar and Sheikh Mehdi perform a *devran* under a picture of the tomb of Pir Ahmad ar-Rifa'i with the emblems of his order: the two flags, the lions the dervishes used to ride, the snakes and scorpions they handle.

49. Women watching Sheikh Mazhar in the *zikr*.

44

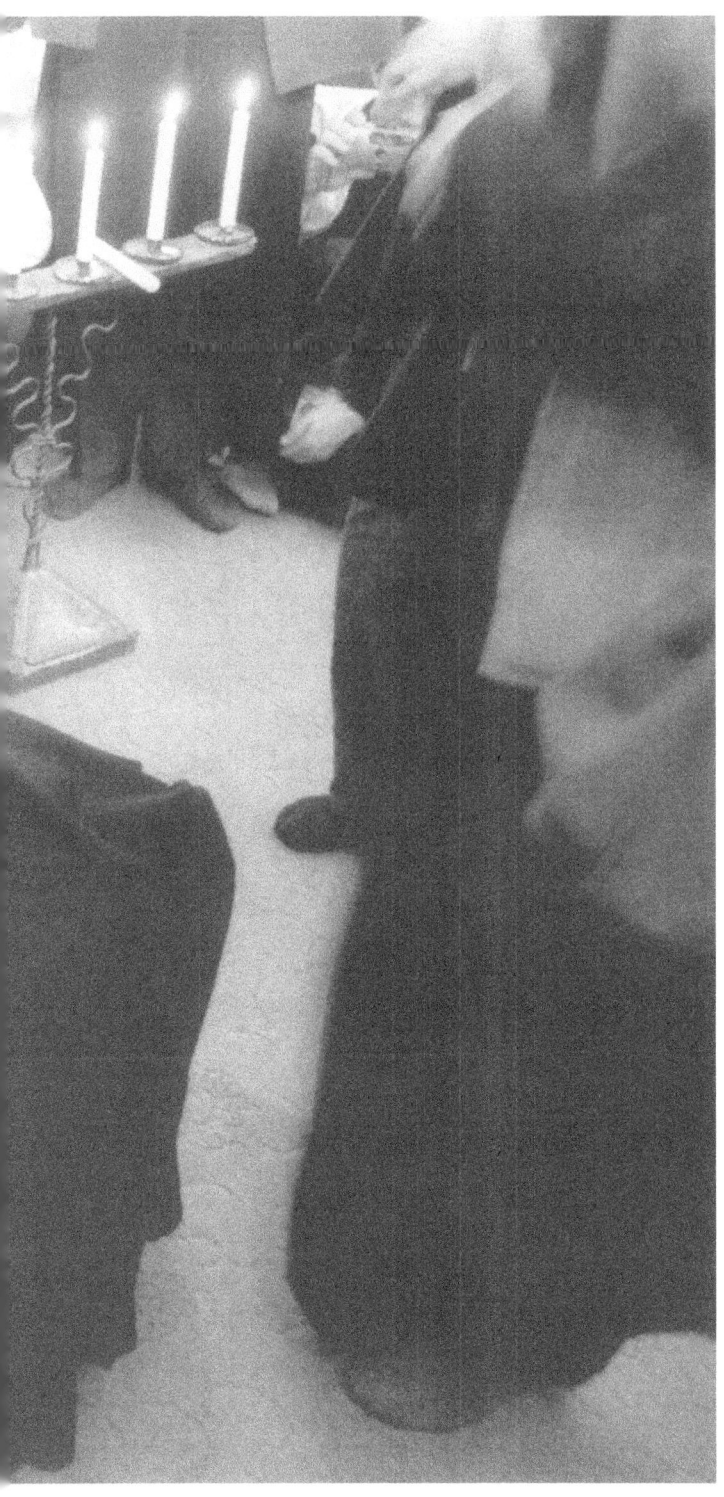

45

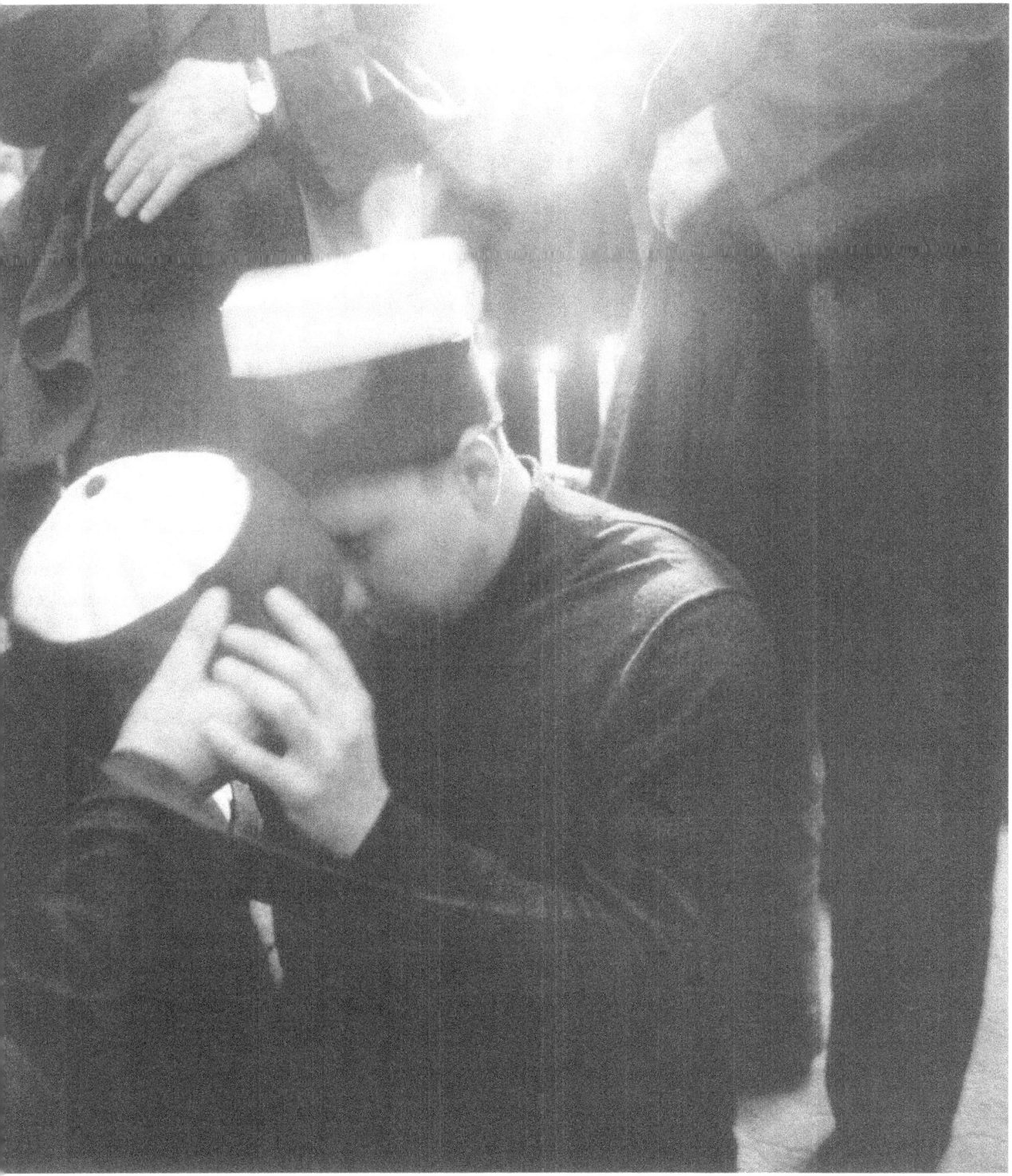

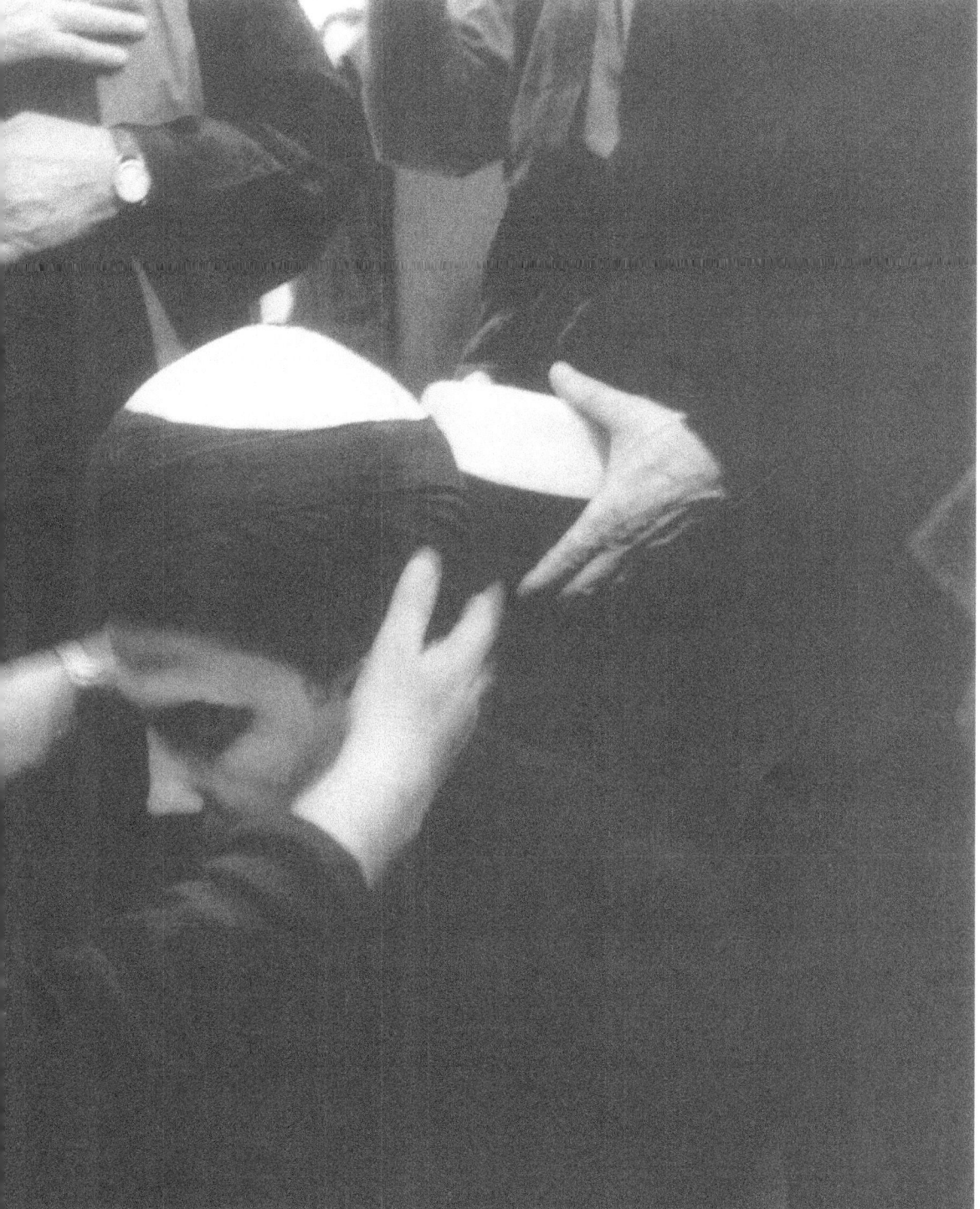

49

50. Sheikh Murtezan in the *turbe* of his *tekke* upon his return from Orahovac, standing beside the tomb of his father, Erol Baba. The *kubur* of Haznadar Baba is on the right, and next to it is the grave of his wife or sister. On the wall is a tapestry showing Ali on his horse brandishing the two-pronged sword *Dhu 'l-Fiqar*. Hanging from the pillar is a thousand-bead rosary. In the foreground are votive candles lit by visitors.

The People

Adem - *one of the dervishes.*

Ali - *the son-in law of the Prophet Muhammad and the supposed founder of Sufism.*

Amdi - *one of the dervishes, and the lead singer in the* zikr. *He is a father of four, and works in a bakery.*

Arben - *one of the dervishes, who is, together with Amdi, responsible for cleaning and maintaining the* turbe. *He is a computer programmer and has one daughter.*

Baba Erol - *the sheikh of this Sufi community until his death in 2005.*

Buyami - *one of the dervishes.*

Haznadar Baba - *the founder of the* tekke *in Skopje, and the principal Muslim saint venerated in Skopje.*

Kerim - *one of the dervishes.*

Pir Ahmad ar-Rifa'i - *the founder of the Rifa'i order.*

Rumi - *Jelal ed-Din Rumi, one of the great Sufi poets and founder of the Mevlevi order.*

Safet - *one of the dervishes.*

Sheikh Mazhar - *the head of the Rifa'i tekke in Djakovica/Gjakova, Kosovo.*

Sheikh Mehdi - *the head of the Rifa'i tekke in Orahovac/Rahovec, Kosovo.*

Sheikh Mustafa Orman - *the head of the Qadiri tekke in Sarajevo.*

Sheikh Murtezan - *the present head of the Rifa'i tekke in Skopje, son of Baba Erol. He is of Turkish ethnicity, and is employed as a professional soldier in the Macedonian army.*

Sheikh Selim - *a Rifa'i sheikh living in Skopje who sometimes visited Baba Erol's tekke.*

Yashar - *one of the dervishes, who normally led the zikr in the absence of Baba Erol. He works in a supermarket.*

Yunus Emre - *One of the first Sufi poets (d. ca. 1320) to use the Turkish language. He is still much loved, and often quoted.*

A green festive flag flying from one of the minarets of the city of Skopje.

The Glossary

Al-Fatiha - the opening chapter of the Koran, somewhat equivalent in use to the Christians' Lord's Prayer.

Amayliya - an amulet.

Ashik - a lover; specifically, a novice.

Ashk - a loving or longing.

Baba - a father, or specifically, a Sufi sheikh.

Batin - the inner meaning of things, known to the mystic.

Bayraktar - a standard bearer; an honorary function for older dervishes in the *tekke*.

Bereket - (Arabic: *baraka*)- blessing connected with a saint or a sacred location.

Dede - in this *tarikat*: a fully initiated dervish.

Def - a tambourine.

Dervish - a Sufi, a Muslim mystic.

Devran - (Arabic: *dawaran*)-a rotating part of the *zikr*.

Dhu 'l-Fiqar - the two-pronged sword of Ali.

Edep - (Arabic: *adab*) - good behaviour.

Ehli Beyt - (Persian: *ahl-i bayt*; Arabic: *ahl al-bayt*) - 'people of the House,' i.e., members of the Prophet's immediate family.

Esma - (Arabic: *asma'*)- names of God and related formulas repeated during the *zikr*.

Ghawth - see *qutb*

Gnosis - mystical knowledge

Hadith- traditions, originally orally transmitted, from the early days of Islam, often about the Prophet Muhammad.

Hakikat - (Arabic: *haqiqa*)- the truth; specifically, the truth about God as revealed to the mystic.

Halka - a circle of dervishes.

Hased - (Arabic: *hasad*)- envy as a source of the Evil Eye.

Haznadar - a treasurer.

Hodža - a teacher in an Islamic school.

Hu-hu-hu -(Arabic: *huwa*)- 'He-He-He', i.e., 'God-God-God'.

'Ibadat - formal duties for the Muslim, like fasting during Ramadan and the five daily prayers.

Ilahi - a hymn sung by the dervishes.

Iman - real faith.

Jubbe - a robe worn by a sheikh.

Kanatlarci - an ethnic Turkish village in south-central Macedonia.

Kemer - a belt worn by a dervish or a sheikh.

Keramet - (Arabic: *karama*) - a miracle.

Khanqah - see *Ribat*; a Persian word for the same institution.

Kiyami - the part of the *zikr* performed standing up.

Kubur or *kabur* - a grave.

Kudret - a force.

Kudum - a hand-held metal percussion instrument.

Kurban - a sacrifice.

Marifet - (Arabic: *ma'rifa*)- intimate knowledge about God.

Mazar - a place to visit; specifically, a holy tomb.

Meded - (Arabic: *madad*)- assistance solicited from a saint.

Mihrab - a niche in a wall indicating the direction of Mecca.

Muabet - (Arabic: *muhabba*) - a friendly conversation after the *zikr*.

Muhib - (Arabic: *muhibb*) - i.e., a lover- a dervish who is not yet fully initiated.

Namaz - the Muslim regular prayer, called *salat* in Arabic.

Qadiri order - a Sufi order, founded by Abdul Qadir al-Jilani.

Oda - a room, e.g., *zikr oda* - a room where the *zikr* takes place.

Pir - a sheikh, specifically the founder of a dervish order.

Qutb - one of the supreme saints who are supposed to rule the world.

Rahovec/Orahovac - a town in the centre of Kosovo.

Rehber - a guide; a dervish who gives guidance to novices.

Ribat - a place where dervishes used to come together before the orders were established.

Rifa'i - a member of the Rifa'i dervish order.

Rifa'i (or Rufa'i) order - a Sufi order, founded by Ahmad ar-Rifa'i.

Roma - present day designation of 'Gypsies'.

Sabr - patience.

Semaana (Persian: *sema'-khane*) - a hall where the *zikr* takes place.

Shefaat - (Arabic: *shafa'a*) - mediation, especially between man and God.

Sheh (Mac.) - see Sheikh.

Shehana - the mother of the sheikh.

Shehzade - a sheikh's son and prospective successor.

Shiis - adherents of the minority branch of Islam (the Shia), prevalent in Iran.

Silsila - the chain of initiations connecting the Sheikh to Ali.

Sheikh - an important man; specifically, the head of an autonomous Sufi group.

Sir - (Arabic: sirr) - the Secret, consisting of private knowledge about the *tarikat* passed from one sheikh to another upon the inauguration of the latter.

Sufism - Islamic mysticism.

Suhbet - see *muabet*.

Sunna - the Prophet's custom, or example.

Sunnis - adherents of the most numerous, "orthodox" branch of Islam.

T'g - a thin pin for the piercing of the cheeks, mostly used with novices and young boys.

Taj - the twelve-furrowed felt cap and turban worn by the Rifa'i sheikhs.

Tarikat (Arabic: *tariqa*, pl. *turuq*) - a dervish order.

Tekke - (Arabic: *takiyya*) - a local centre of a Sufi order, headed by a sheikh.

Tesbih or *tespih* - a rosary with 33, 99, 100, 999, 1000 or even 5000 beads used in prayer and for other ritual purposes.

Thousand-bead rosary - a rosary with one thousand beads used in prayer, and passed over the heads of supplicants at the holy tomb.

Turbe - a building housing one or more holy tombs.

'Ulama' - pl. of *'alim*, Islamic jurists

Vekil - a deputy; significantly, a sheikh's deputy. Sometimes upon the death of a sheikh no successor is inaugurated, and the *tekke* can be run by one or more *vekils* for years.

Vekil-zakirbashi - a dervish who leads the *zikr* in the absence of the sheikh.

Veli, pl. *evliya* - (Arabic: *wali*, Pl. *awliya'*)- a 'friend of God', i.e., a Muslim saint.

Vird or *evrad* - (Arabic: *wird*, pl. *awrad*)-a litany, often sung as a warming-up to the *zikr*.

Votive candles - candles lighted near a holy tomb to underscore one's requests from a saint.

Zahir - visible

Zarp - an iron pin with a wooden handle for the piecing of cheeks and other parts of the body during the *zikr*. The word is derived from *darb es-silah*, the Arabic term for the piercing.

Zikr - (Arabic: *dhikr*)-the act of remembering (God); the main Sufi ritual.

Zil - cymbals.

Ziyaret- (Arabic: *ziyara*) a visit to a holy tomb.

For Product Safety Concerns and Information please contact our EU representative GPSR@taylorandfrancis.com
Taylor & Francis Verlag GmbH, Kaufingerstraße 24, 80331 München, Germany

www.ingramcontent.com/pod-product-compliance
Lightning Source LLC
Chambersburg PA
CBHW080940300426
44115CB00017B/2890